P9-CLA-261

Praise for

The Official BRIGHT LINE EATING Cookbook

"This is absolutely unlike any other cookbook. Dr. Thompson offers an opportunity
for a new relationship with food based on research showing that a simple diet is the
foundation for permanent weight loss. Inside you will find delicious, nutritious, simple
meals to help the brain heal from food addiction and lower the adiposity set point.
Meaning no more yo-yo dieting. No more pain of regain. For the generations whose
brains were hijacked by refined foods, Bright Line Eating is truly a revolution."

— **MARK HYMAN, M.D.,**
director, Cleveland Center for Functional Medicine and #1 *New York Times*
best-selling author of *Food: What the Heck Should I Eat?*

"If you struggle with food, your weight, addictive eating, and are just
plain tired of trying to decide what to eat, then Bright Line Eating
could be the best decision you've ever made."

— **CHRISTIANE NORTHRUP, M.D.,**
New York Times best-selling author of *Goddesses Never Age,*
The Wisdom of Menopause, and *Women's Bodies, Women's Wisdom*

"I've referred tens of thousands of people to Bright Line Eating, and they've collectively
released more than 100,000 pounds. The fact is, this program works like nothing ever
developed in the history of weight loss. And now, with her brilliant cookbook,
Dr. Susan Peirce Thompson has made it easier than ever to put it into practical and
delicious action. Whether you're omnivorous or (more power to you!) plant-powered,
you'll find recipes to support you in easily implementing your bright lines,
finding food freedom, and moving in healthier directions. Bon appétit!"

— **OCEAN ROBBINS,**
co-founder and CEO, Food Revolution Network
and author of *31-Day Food Revolution*

Also by

SUSAN PEIRCE THOMPSON, Ph.D.

BRIGHT LINE EATING:
The Science of Living Happy, Thin, and Free

The above is available at your local bookstore,
or may be ordered by visiting:

Hay House USA: www.hayhouse.com®
Hay House Australia: www.hayhouse.com.au
Hay House UK: www.hayhouse.co.uk
Hay House India: www.hayhouse.co.in

The Official

BRIGHT
LINE
EATING
Cookbook

The Official
BRIGHT
LINE
EATING
Cookbook

WEIGHT
LOSS
Made
Simple

SUSAN PEIRCE THOMPSON, Ph.D.

HAY
HOUSE

HAY HOUSE, INC.

Carlsbad, California • New York City
London • Sydney • New Delhi

Copyright © 2019 by Susan Peirce Thompson, Ph.D.

Published in the United States by: Hay House, Inc.: www.hayhouse.com®
Published in Australia by: Hay House Australia Pty. Ltd.: www.hayhouse.com.au
Published in the United Kingdom by: Hay House UK, Ltd.: www.hayhouse.co.uk
Published in India by: Hay House Publishers India: www.hayhouse.co.in

Indexer: Joan Shapiro
Cover design: Amy Rose Grigoriou
Interior design: Charles McStravick

Recipe photography by Alan De Herrera
All other interior photos used under license from Shutterstock.com

All rights reserved. No part of this book may be reproduced by any mechanical, photographic, or electronic process, or in the form of a phonographic recording; nor may it be stored in a retrieval system, transmitted, or otherwise be copied for public or private use—other than for "fair use" as brief quotations embodied in articles and reviews—without prior written permission of the publisher.

The author of this book does not dispense medical advice or prescribe the use of any technique as a form of treatment for physical, emotional, or medical problems without the advice of a physician, either directly or indirectly. The intent of the author is only to offer information of a general nature to help you in your quest for emotional, physical, and spiritual well-being. In the event you use any of the information in this book for yourself, the author and the publisher assume no responsibility for your actions.

Cataloging-in-Publication Data is on file at the Library of Congress.

Hardcover ISBN: 978-1-4019-5713-1
e-book ISBN: 978-1-4019-5714-8
e-audio ISBN: 978-1-4019-5852-7

10 9 8 7 6 5 4 3 2 1
1st edition, October 2019

PRINTED IN THE UNITED STATES OF AMERICA

SUSTAINABLE FORESTRY INITIATIVE
Certified Chain of Custody
Promoting Sustainable Forestry
www.sfiprogram.org
SFI-01268

SFI label applies to the text stock

Contents

Introduction

Welcome to a cookbook unlike any you've ever used before. This is not your typical "diet" cookbook where you can just skip ahead to the recipes, follow the weekly meal plan, cross your fingers, and hope that this time you're going to lose your excess weight—and keep it off. That's because Bright Line Eating is not your typical weight-loss program. The typical weight-loss program has a financial model based on recidivism. According to a study published in the *American Journal of Public Health,* fewer than 1 percent of obese people are able to achieve a normal BMI within one year.* And 78 percent of those who lose at least 5 percent of their body weight regain it within five years.[1] In essence, across all people and all programs, diets have a 99 percent failure rate. If you have thought maybe it's just you, it isn't.

Everyone who comes to Bright Line Eating has already tried some form of diet or weight-loss program. In fact, our research shows that the average Bright Liner has made more than 16 attempts to rid themselves of their excess weight; their constant cravings; and the endless bargaining, obsessing, and sabotage we are all familiar with. Nothing has worked. Some of us have spent thousands of dollars on conventional weight-loss programs, only to have to reenroll and reenroll and reenroll . . . and still whatever weight we have lost always comes back—and then some.

We are not alone.

In the United States, more than 70 percent of people are overweight or obese.[2] Nearly half of our white children and adolescents are overweight or obese, as are nearly three-quarters of our children and adolescents of color.[3] That excess weight comes with dire health consequences: 1.5 million new cases of type 2 diabetes are diagnosed each year,[4] resulting in 84,000 people getting a foot or leg amputated annually,[5] and 63 percent of us are dying early from obesity-related diseases.[6]

Additionally, long before we die from eating this way, we stop living. I remember vividly what it felt like to be obese. It was mentally and physically exhausting. On my way to becoming the speaker for my graduating class at UC Berkeley, I would lumber across campus with marshmallows in my pocket, needing a "fix" every few minutes just to keep going. It was misery. And therein lies the paradox that led me on this field of inquiry, and ultimately to creating Bright Line Eating: I could get myself to do everything I needed to do to graduate with highest honors and start (and then finish) my Ph.D. in Brain and Cognitive Sciences, but I could not control my eating.

---

* Candidates for bariatric surgery are advised that their "excess weight" is the difference between their current weight and the weight that would correspond to a BMI of 25, which corresponds to the upper limit of the "normal" classification. For the average person desiring to reach their ideal weight, the target BMI is closer to 21. For the average person joining a Bright Line Eating Boot Camp, their excess weight is approximately 35 percent of their body weight.

The reason, I ultimately discovered, is that our bodies did not evolve to be able to process modern "food." What we have been putting in our mouths since the end of World War II is hijacking our brains until they are rewired to block every attempt at losing weight. The frustrating obstacle that creates that depressing one percent statistic is actually inside our own heads!

To free your brain from this hostage situation is no small feat. I would propose that it is the fight of a lifetime. But at Bright Line Eating, we are winning it.

It has been two and a half years since my first book, *Bright Line Eating*, was published. In that time, thousands more people have joined our Boot Camp and generously shared their data. Thanks to their contributions, I now know even more about the road to living "Happy, Thin, and Free."

What I've learned is that for people who have struggled with their weight their entire lives, the forces of Sad, Obese, and Food Obsessed are going to put up a major fight. A brain rewired by the "food" we have available today is not going to go gently or give up easily. When I designed Bright Line Eating, I built into it a ton of support and resources. What we've learned is that the people who lean into this support and "stay close to the Mothership" do best. They lose their excess weight more quickly and achieve the greatest freedom by surrendering wholly to this new way of eating.

Teaching people new to Bright Line Eating *how* to eat this way is the next best level of support I can offer.

That said, I am now going to declare something that may seem quite strange at the opening of a cookbook: Bright Line Eating is not about food. Lots of diets have food plans. Many of them are pretty similar. Most are fine and fairly healthy. In fact, many people come to Bright Line Eating from diets loaded with whole, plant-based foods. They are eating a lot of vegetables and have a high-nutrient diet—but they are intractably overweight or obese and still addicted to food.

What differentiates Bright Line Eating from everything else out there is the program itself. In the next chapter I will recap, in brief, the four Bright Lines and the highlights of the program. But first, for you to get a baseline of your personal food picture and how best to use this book, go to www.foodfreedomquiz.com and take the 5-minute Food Freedom Quiz, which will measure where you land on the

10-point Susceptibility Scale. This is a metric I devised that helps people quantify the pull that refined foods have on them.

For those of you who score a 6 or above, know that just getting this recap of the Bright Lines and the program highlights most likely will not be enough for you to get—and stay—at goal weight. For you, I highly encourage getting online and joining one of our Boot Camps. No need to travel; you can do it from home. All you need is Internet access. If that isn't feasible, get your hands on the first book and read it in its entirety. I don't need you to buy it—get it at the library or borrow it from a friend. But I want you to succeed with my whole heart. What the research shows is that if you have a brain that is highly susceptible to the pull of addictive foods, you need to take advantage of ALL the science, ALL the support structures built into the program, and ALL the information on HOW to do Bright Line Eating. If I were to include that here, this book would be 1,500 pages.

My most earnest entreaty is simply this: Do not shortchange yourself. Do not let this be one more thing you tried and failed.

The purpose of this cookbook is to go into far more depth explaining the food itself than I have done before, and to share wisdom culled from thousands of Bright Lifers to make your meal prep as easy as possible. (Bright Lifers are what we call people who have graduated from the BLE Boot Camp and then committed not only to living Happy, Thin, and Free for the rest of their lives, but also to staying close to the Mothership to keep their lines strong and shiny.) We are all here to help you, and this cookbook is our gift to you. We never want anyone to feel overwhelmed by the process of shifting to this new way of eating and use that as an excuse to not make this life-saving change. If *"What do I eat???"* feels like an insurmountable mental challenge, this book is here to solve that problem for you. It is all laid out so if you want to relinquish all decision-making on your path to Food Freedom, you can. You can follow the meal plans in Part III for the duration of your weight loss if you'd like. Or, you can use our recipes to add variety to what you're eating already. Either way, we've got you covered.

You are also going to get tons of food prep and food management advice in Part II, collected from our community of Bright Lifers and vetted by our scientists. The advice is designed to support you on every step of your journey, especially around the wild world of vegetables, which may be wholly new terrain for you. I promise you there are no new questions—if you are facing a challenge, someone ahead of you has solved it. Benefit from their experience.

At the end of every chapter, you will meet some of our Bright Lifers—read their stories and see their before-and-after pictures. They are sharing their case studies with you because they want you to know they were once exactly where you are now—cynical, hopeful, dubious, desperate—and they made it to the other side. They surrendered to the plan and now, as you will see by their faces, they are truly living Happy, Thin, and Free.

A note about the framework of the book. In Part II, the recipes are categorized in a way that might seem strange to you now. One of our Bright Lines is Meals: We eat only three a day with nothing in between.* We call them breakfast, lunch, and dinner, like everyone else. But that is where the similarities end. Our food tends to fall into four categories: breakfasts, plates, cold bowls, and warm bowls. The bowls have evolved because over time we found that, instead of making a plate with

---

* Some Bright Lifers have modified their plan to include fewer or more meals than three a day (two, four, five, etc.) and that is still fully Bright Line–compliant, so long as all food is eaten as a preplanned meal with no grazing or snacking in between.

distinct servings of protein, vegetables (raw and/or cooked), grain, fruit, and fat, people were dumping everything together into one delicious dish frequently eaten in a large bowl. In fact, at the latest annual Bright Line Eating Family Reunion, many people packed their big wooden salad bowls in their suitcases!

We must say, though, that within this framework there is tremendous flexibility. So although we present Cold Bowls as "Likely Lunch" and Warm Bowls as the "Dinner Domain," it is true that some people prefer cooked vegetables and will therefore eat a warm bowl at lunch. Some people in hotter climates enjoy cold bowls across the board. Some people stick with the kind of recipes you'll find in the "Perfect Plates" chapter. But any of these may be used for your lunch or dinner as long as you are following your food plan and have the right quantity of protein, vegetables, grain, fruit, and fat recommended for you at that meal.

The recipes are configured for a woman's weight-loss food plan. We want to make a note here about the vegetable quantities in the recipes. The standard weight-loss plan calls for 6 ounces of vegetables at lunch and 14 ounces of vegetables at dinner, and all vegetables can be either raw or cooked. However, many Bright Line Eaters modify those 20 ounces of daily vegetables into 10 ounces at lunch and 10 ounces at dinner, for simplicity. Also, we have some who follow a plan that allows for more than 20 ounces of vegetables per day. The good news is that none of the recipes will suffer if you add more vegetables or if you take away some vegetables from the recipe as written so that it conforms to your plan. Just weigh out your ounces before serving.

We will also include portion and adaptation guidelines for men, who need more protein and more calories on average. For people who have lost all their excess weight and are now living on the Maintenance Plan (which has more whole grains), we will cover what I call the "dance of maintenance" in depth in the "Getting to Goal Weight" section at the end of Chapter 2. But for now, the basic concept is that you get a bit more food when you're at maintenance and no longer have to lose weight. For example, you might eat a grilled tofu and peppers recipe exactly as presented when you are losing your excess weight, but once you reach Maintenance you might serve it over rice.

You'll find the recipes in this book to be a little different than what you may be used to. As Bright Line Eaters, we eat an exact amount of vegetables, grains, fruits, proteins, and fat. It's very simple to manage when each item is cooked separately. For example, we can put 6 ounces of cooked vegetables, like roasted squash, on our plate, along with 4 ounces of meat or 6 ounces of beans, add our fat serving and a piece of fruit, and we are all set. Easy peasy!

Loading our plates becomes a little more complicated to manage when using recipes that combine foods from different groups. By mixing things together, we have to think a bit harder to make sure we have the right amount of each. There are many recipes in this book that keep it simple by not combining food groups, but there are also many that do. We've tried to make even these as simple as possible for you by including instructions on how to end up with the right amount of each food group on your plate.

In some cases, you will be instructed to cook items separately and then combine them after weighing. In other cases, all the food will be cooked together, but you'll start with measured quantities of the critical ingredients, so the number of servings is accurate.

Finally, even with simple recipes, sometimes the serving size is known, but the total number of servings the recipe yields is not. For example, the serving size of Ratatouille is 6 ounces, but we don't know how many 6-ounce servings the recipe will make because some zucchini are bigger than others. In those cases, the number of servings simply says "Multiple."

For simplicity, most dishes make a 6-ounce serving of cooked veggies, which can count as the total lunch portion of vegetables or the dinner portion of cooked vegetables. When using one of these recipes at dinner time, add an 8-ounce salad to complete the 14-ounce vegetable portion for dinner.

At the end, in Part III, we'll present weekly and monthly meal plans for those of you who want to take all the decision making out of your weight-loss journey. These are just suggestions. Feel free to swap out any of the recipes listed for something else in this book you prefer. There is truly something here to satisfy everyone, no matter their flavor preferences or dietary restrictions. You hate broccoli? You don't ever have to eat it. You prefer paleo? Bright Line Eating can adapt.

I know it sounds like a lot to figure out, but once you have eaten this way for a few weeks it will start to become automatic and then, eventually, it will feel very strange *not* to eat this way. Along the journey, you'll gradually be getting into a right-sized body, perhaps one that is pain-free for the first time in years or off of all its various medications. We see this all the time. This is why you'll be hearing directly from Bright Lifers throughout these pages—people who once felt completely hopeless but who now live full, vibrant, *easy* lives.

I'll leave you with this: The fact is that losing weight is exhausting. By definition, it requires eating fewer calories than you expend, which forces your body to undergo the effortful task of harvesting fuel from within. Plus, since fat cells store our toxins, shrinking them dumps waste into our bloodstream, making us very tired. Not fun. Which is why I want you to have to do it only one more time—*ever*.

Then I want you to stay at your goal weight for the rest of your life.

It is truly, realistically possible.

Five years in, what we're seeing is that BLE is unusually, outrageously successful *for the people who continue to do it*—the people who commit their food daily, keep their Bright Lines shiny, and surrender to the plan as it was designed. But if you cut corners at the beginning, or give it a good start and then succumb to the overconfidence bias and drift away, the weight will return, along with the disappointment, the joint pain, and the despair.

Those of us who succeed follow the formula. We *trust* the plan and really *do* it. We let go of our old ways of relating to food, conceptualizing food, and using food. We realize that if we had known how to succeed we would have done it already. So we embrace this new way of eating wholeheartedly, allowing these new habits to reshape our brains. At the same time, we *invest* in this community. This places us in an environment where our new way, which flies in the face of our entire food culture, is normalized, reinforced, and refreshed all the time. Because society, which we are all still a part of, works to erode our resolve DAILY. So we have to replenish it daily as well.

Starting right now, you are a part of our community. Let us help you become everything you were meant to be. Let us help you live Happy, Thin, and Free.

BETSY MEYNARDIE

Before

After

STARTING DATE **January 24, 2017**
HEAVIEST WEIGHT **260 pounds**
STARTING WEIGHT **250 pounds**
GOAL WEIGHT ACHIEVED **July 2, 2018**
CURRENT WEIGHT **148 pounds**
HEIGHT **5'7"**

*W*hen I started BLE in January of 2017, I wasn't sure I could do it. I'm one of those people who have tried almost every diet out there. I've always been successful at losing the weight, but never at keeping it off. Recently, I'd ballooned up to almost my highest weight and felt physically horrible, unhappy with how I looked, and mad at myself for failing again. Without a lot of confidence that I could manage no sugar or flour for the long term, I joined a Bright Line Eating Boot Camp. I took the mantra, "One day at a time," to heart and was able to keep my lines bright. It took me a year and a half to release more than 100 pounds, and now I'm on maintenance. What I wasn't expecting is how much I've changed on this journey.

I had never really cooked before. I just went to the fridge or pantry and found something or ate a lot of frozen meals. Now I'm a person who cooks and prepares meals: simple, easy ones that work for me.

I used to snack and graze all day long. Now I'm a person who doesn't snack and I'm not constantly thinking about food.

I rarely bought vegetables. Now my shopping cart is always full of fresh produce.

Before BLE, bags of salad would often go bad in my fridge. Now I shop for veggies twice a week and I eat up everything I buy.

I was always the one who brought drinks or paper products to potlucks. Now people ask for my roasted vegetables or huge signature salad.

My confidence has grown with my new identity as a Bright Lifer. I kept all my large-size clothes for over a year because I didn't have the confidence that I wouldn't need them again. Now I embrace this identity and know that with the support I have in the program, this is my life for the future. In addition to releasing my weight, now I have released pounds of my large-size clothes. I know I'm not going to need them again.

Perhaps most important, I've changed from a person on a weight-loss program to a person who doesn't eat sugar and flour. My language has changed from "I can't eat that" to "I don't eat that." I enjoy my BLE meals a lot and love the freedom I have from mind chatter around food. I will forever be grateful to Bright Line Eating and the BLE community.

Part One

The Revolutionary Neuroscience of Sustainable Weight Loss

Chapter 1

Why Bright Line Eating Works

Before we can discuss the four Bright Lines and how to implement them, we need to quickly recap what is happening in the brain that blocks weight loss in the first place. We're going to begin by talking about something most overweight people are probably sick of hearing about: willpower. But hang on, because most people have absolutely no idea what willpower really is.

WHAT IS WILLPOWER?

As I wrote in my first book, when I taught college courses in Introductory Psychology and the Psychology of Eating, I would always ask my students, "What do you think willpower is?" The majority mistakenly said it's a quality that you're born with or some kind of barometer of the strength of your intention to do (or not do) something. And so believe most of the people who start our Bright Line Eating Boot Camp each week.

I am guessing you are going to be very relieved to hear that it's neither.

Willpower is actually just a brain function that originates in the anterior cingulate cortex. Interestingly, this mechanism is not only in charge of resisting temptation; it also governs our ability to focus, monitor task performance, regulate emotions, and, most important, make decisions. Which means you're taxing your anterior cingulate cortex when you pay attention at a staff meeting, proof a report, keep your patience with your kids, and decide how to handle each of those 17 emails in your inbox. Here is the important piece: Exerting self-control in one area of our lives exhausts this finite resource and prevents self-regulation in other areas.[1]

Which is why, in my opinion, weight-loss programs that recommend simultaneously starting "diet and exercise" set people up for failure. The dieters deplete their willpower first thing in the morning by hitting the gym and then overeat later. Does this sound familiar?

It's vital to understand this, because most of us naturally have only about 15 minutes of effective self-regulatory capacity at a time.* Fifteen minutes. Can you imagine if your phone only had 15 minutes of charge?

And it gets worse: When glucose levels drop in the anterior cingulate cortex, activity in this area virtually stops.[2] So at the end of a long day when blood sugar levels are at their lowest, our brains are truly incapable of making a wise choice about what to eat.

And once again, we fall into the Willpower Gap.

---

* In several studies, a 15-minute exposure to temptation was enough for a large number of the subjects to have impaired performance on a subsequent task.

What this looks like is starting the day with great intentions, only to end up eating a donut out of the break room after a stressful meeting and telling yourself, *Oh, well, I'll start again tomorrow.*

This is why any diet that expects willpower to get you across the finish line and beyond is ludicrous.

As I often say, what we all need is a plan that assumes we have no willpower at all—because at any given moment we may not—and works anyway. Most important, once we've learned the scientific reality of the Willpower Gap, we can finally stop thinking we are fundamentally flawed. The fact is that limitations arising from the way willpower is wired in the brain will consistently leave you vulnerable to unhelpful food choices.

But that's not all. At that point, something even worse happens.

Those unhelpful food choices set off a cascade of activity in your brain that creates two things: insatiable hunger and overpowering cravings.

INSATIABLE HUNGER

Evolutionarily, insatiable hunger is a new kind of hunger. It's not a survival drive to consume fuel so that we can hunt, gather, build shelter, and procreate. It's more like, "I just ate dinner and finished my kids' dinner and now I'm eating a few pieces of candy while I do the dishes and then I'm going to head to the freezer for ice cream." *Insatiable* hunger.

Scientists have noticed that insatiable hunger differs from real hunger in two key ways. The first is that it's accompanied by a strong urge to be sedentary. The second is that eating doesn't actually satiate it.

All very peculiar. The scientist in me wanted to understand what this was about, even as I was in its grips. For thousands of years, though diets developed differently across the globe, in general we were a species, like all other animals, that effortlessly took in roughly the sustenance we needed to survive. So what had broken? Why did my brain suddenly think I needed *so much more*?

It turns out that the crux of the problem stems from what eating these new, calorically dense, nutritionally empty "foods" at all times of day is doing to our brains.

LEPTIN

In 1949, a group of mice born in a lab didn't behave like normal mice—they didn't scurry or dart about.[3] Instead, they sat and ate until they became morbidly obese. Eventually, in 1994, scientists discovered that the mice had been born without the hormone leptin.[4] This is the hormone that tells us that we're full and need to move. Once the mice were injected with leptin, they became totally uninterested in excess food and jumped on their wheels and got thin.

This of course led science (and pharmaceutical companies) down a rabbit hole of artificial leptin manufacturing. But what is interesting about overweight humans, however, is that we are not lacking leptin. In fact, overweight people have *more* leptin in their blood than slender people. So, what's happening? Why the leptin resistance? Why are we sedentary and forever hungry? Why can't the overweight system recognize its own leptin? The answer is that leptin is being blocked in the brain.

By insulin.[5]

The sugar in our diet is elevating insulin levels far beyond where our bodies were intended to idle. Research on overweight kids has shown that their average insulin levels rise 45 percent between grade school and high school,[6] which is creating a surge in type 2 diabetes.

And that's not all that sugar is doing to us.

OVERPOWERING CRAVINGS

Overpowering cravings may seem very similar to insatiable hunger. And while the net result of both is that we end up eating more food than our bodies need, they're not the same thing.

Insatiable hunger, caused by leptin resistance, is what drives people to mindlessly put food in their mouth all day—in other words, graze. Overpowering cravings, on the other hand, are the bingeing mechanism. It's eating a whole jar of peanut butter or a full bag of Oreo cookies. Overpowering cravings are what make people, myself included, drive miles out of their way for that one specific food—their fix—just to scratch that itch in their brain.

But where does that itch originate?

THE NUCLEUS ACCUMBENS

The nucleus accumbens is a cluster of neurons activated by dopamine and designed to motivate our behavior with rewards, which is why so many life-sustaining activities stimulate the brain to release dopamine: sex, physical exertion, and, yes, eating. Of course, this is also the seat of addiction. Our brains simply weren't designed to process the modern chemical flood we can get from porn, drugs, or donuts. When you start pumping that much dopamine into the nucleus accumbens, it protects itself from the overstimulation by downregulating.

DOWNREGULATION

Downregulation is an adaptive process. When the brain is hit with an onslaught of stimuli, say from PornHub or Cinnabon, the brain thins out the dopamine receptors in an effort to adapt to the overload so that the next time a sensory tsunami comes, the response will be more manageable.

The problem is that now you're changing the physiology of the brain. If the stimulation is not forthcoming, you don't feel very good. In high school, long before I became a Ph.D. in Brain and Cognitive Sciences, I was a crystal meth addict who dropped out of high school and became a crack cocaine addict. With incredible help and grace, I was able to kick both addictions before I was even legally old enough to buy the alcohol I no longer wanted or ever touched again. But food was harder. Food was an addiction that took me years and years and years more to finally kick. But what I will say about drugs is this: They virtually wipe out the dopamine

receptors in the nucleus accumbens. And, after a certain point, getting high didn't feel pleasurable or even good. It just felt like I needed *more.*

Once the dopamine downregulation kicked in, the state I was forced to tolerate between fixes was the extreme *absence* of pleasure. Pretty soon I needed more . . . not to get high, but to get *normal.* This is something I think a lot of people misunderstand. They think the addict is using to feel good, but really the addict is using just to be okay for a bit.

When it comes to food, it's the same story. Sugar didn't enter our diets until the 1700s. Our bodies and brains never really adapted to process it well. For a long time that was okay, because for hundreds of years it was expensive and only people of means, like nobility, could afford it.

With the advent of the sugar plantation, all that changed. Then, as we all know, over the last few decades of global trade, terribly misguided federal subsidies, and progressively more ingenious snack food manufacturing, sugar consumption has increased dramatically, and that means that we are hitting our brains with ever higher, ever more potent levels of stimulation. We are flooding the receptors with dopamine and they are thinning out. From a neurological perspective, the research is very clear. We need to stop looking at the culprits as food and start thinking of them as what they really are: drugs.

SUGAR AND FLOUR IN THE BRAIN

Cocaine comes from the coca leaf of South America. Hikers in the Andes Mountains chew on these leaves, making their cheeks a little numb and giving them a little lift, like drinking a cup of caffeinated tea. Has anyone ever committed a violent crime to get more coca leaves? No. And research has actually proven that coca leaves, on their own, are not addictive.[7] But when you take the *inner essence* of those coca leaves and refine and purify that inner essence into a fine powder, you now have a very powerful drug.[8]

Heroin comes from the poppy plant. If you sit in a field and eat poppies all day you'll fail a urine test for opium, but you're not going to become an itchy, desperate heroin addict. It's only when you take the inner essence of that poppy plant and refine and purify it into a fine powder that you get the drug called heroin.

Next is sugar. We get sugar from the sugarcane plant, as well as beets, rice, corn, and coconuts—all foods I eat freely. (I could probably even chew on a stalk of sugarcane, but it would involve a little travel and a very strong jaw.) But, when you take the inner essence of those plants and you refine and purify it into a powder or thick liquid, now you have a drug. You've taken a food and you've turned it into a drug.

And finally, flour. Where do you get flour from? Well, any number of plants, including grains, tubers, nuts, and legumes—all healthy foods, in their whole form. But when you take their inner essence and refine and purify it into a fine powdery substance, you now have created a drug.

I provide much more research evidence in my first book, but know that science has proven that food addiction is real. As real as cocaine or heroin addiction. There is no physiological difference. Have you ever made a rational decision to turn away from foods that are harming you, *but then found yourself eating them anyway?* That's addiction. People ask me, "Really, sugar and flour are as addictive as cocaine and heroin?" Actually, researchers estimate that they might be *more* addictive.

THE DOWNREGULATED LIFE

Dr. Robert Lustig of the University of California, San Francisco, is one of the leading experts on the effects of sugar. He describes how it takes only three weeks of consistent overstimulation for the dopamine receptors in our brain to thin out.[9] Once that happens, addiction takes hold. Meaning, first, that life in between eating the stimulating foods feels bleak, which is one of the links between the Standard American Diet and depression. Second, the ability to taste food actually diminishes.[10] In addition, studies have shown that the anticipation of food in the brain of an obese person is much stronger than a slender person, but when they eat, their pleasure is *lower.*[11] In other words, if you're on one of those diets I discussed in the Introduction, and you start to think about how amazing it would be to eat something off your plan, your brain will exaggerate the upcoming payoff. If you actually eat it, that payoff won't come; you'll just be left craving the next hit.

I used to live like that. In my early 20s, I remember driving to the all-night supermarket to scavenge the aisles for cookie-dough ingredients, pints of ice cream, and bags of chips, going home to eat compulsively for hours, waiting for some feeling that never came. I wanted to feel full. I wanted to feel done. I would finish—the bowl, the bag, the pint—but I was never done.

Until I was done with sugar and flour completely.

THE WAY OUT

I can hear you. "Wait—what? Done with sugar and flour???" Perhaps that is such an overwhelming concept that your mind is drawing a blank as to what that life would even look like . . . as if I just said, "Give up air." That is part of the mission of this cookbook—to show you that there is so much wonderful, delicious, nourishing food that doesn't contain any sugar or flour. Eating this way has worked for me for a long time now, and I have seen it work sustainably for thousands of others around the world.

But the parts of your brain that have been hijacked by sugar and flour are going to put up a huge fight. They want you to find the "diet" that will let them keep getting their fix while somehow getting you into a right-sized body. If you ever find it please let me know.

Maybe you were given this book by someone who has lost—and kept off—100 pounds, or more. Someone who is off all their diabetes medication, their cholesterol meds, their antidepressants, and their anti-inflammatories for their knee pain. Someone who is living life like they never have before. Maybe you know one of us personally and you want some of that for yourself. I hope so.

Enter Bright Lines.

The most important contribution of the Bright Lines is that they bridge the Willpower Gap. Bright Lines give you clear rules for what you do—and don't—put in your mouth. And the result is that eating foods that are good for you becomes automatic. You don't have to think about it. There's no decision to make. It doesn't matter that it's 4 P.M. and you have a tray of donuts in front of you. You will stand there knowing *exactly* what you are going to eat next, and those donuts aren't it. The purpose of the Bright Lines is to enable you to stop thinking about food, and to stop grappling with the 221 food-related choices the average person has to make in a day.[12] There is only one choice—respect the Bright Lines.

Bright Line Eating, as I designed it, is a commitment to follow four Bright Lines we never cross: Sugar, Flour, Meals, and Quantities. I'm going to outline each Bright Line in depth and explain the science behind why it works.

1: SUGAR

This is the keystone Bright Line, without which none of the others stand a chance, because only by taking sugar out of the equation can the brain and body heal.

This means eliminating sugar in all its forms: cane sugar, beet sugar, date sugar, brown sugar, powdered sugar, evaporated cane juice, rice syrup, corn syrup, high-fructose corn syrup, honey, agave, maple syrup, molasses, sucrose, dextrose (indeed, anything ending in *ose*), maltitol, malted barley extract, maltodextrin, saccharine, NutraSweet, aspartame, sucralose, xylitol, sorbitol, and, yes, stevia and Truvía.

It might surprise you to read that artificial sweetener is also out of bounds. But studies have repeatedly shown that artificial sweeteners will absolutely derail your weight loss. Artificial sweeteners mimic a starvation state in the brain, leading to a 50 percent increase in food consumption.[13] They also destroy your gut microbiome and lead to glucose dysregulation.[14] In addition, many of the products containing artificial sweeteners, like diet soda and sugarless gum, will keep you hooked on the behavior of putting something sweet in your mouth as a crutch to get through the day. Let them go.

2: FLOUR

The second Bright Line is Flour. For people high on the Susceptibility Scale, flour is this very sneaky seductress that hides behind so many mythologies to keep people overweight. "I bake homemade bread." "Baking was a huge part of how we bonded as a family." "My mother made her own pasta—from scratch."

"It's whole grain." "It's high in fiber." "It's health bread!" So many people come into Bright Line Eating having experimented with giving up sugar, only to watch their flour consumption, and their weight, balloon. The science of flour addiction is in its infancy. We know that flour raises insulin levels,[15] but we haven't uncovered the dopamine connection. YET. But no one has ever driven out in the rain at 3 A.M. to get sauce and cheese on broccoli. Why do people rate pizza as the *number one* most addictive food in existence?[16] It's the flour.

Just as with sugar, the Bright Line for flour covers ALL flour. It's not about the type of plant. It's not about gluten. It's not about "whole grain." It's about *surface area*. When the food is processed, the surface area gets multiplied exponentially and the resulting molecules hit the system too fast and too hard.

3: MEALS

Eliminating sugar and flour is a good start, but if that's all you do, odds are you won't be successful long term. Eventually you'll fall prey to the Willpower Gap and your efforts won't last. This is where Meals, the third Bright Line, comes in. When regular meals become part of the scaffolding of your life, it takes the burden off willpower. When you set up a schedule of eating three meals a day at regular meal-times (breakfast at breakfast time, lunch at lunchtime, and dinner at dinnertime) and in a designated place that is not your car, your couch, or your multiplex—not only does eating the right things become automatic, but passing up the wrong things in between also becomes automatic.

4: QUANTITIES

The fourth and final Bright Line is Quantities. This is the Bright Line that clicks everything into place and ensures that your weight will melt off and leave you in a right-sized body. It works even if you're postmenopausal, on medications that increase your hunger, genetically predisposed to obesity, struggling with hypo-thyroidism, or, like me once, pregnant with twins. Don't worry, the Bright Line for quantities is your safety net.

The quantities of Bright Line meals are generous, but they are finite. What this does is take your judgment out of the equation and ensure your sustained weight loss.

I recommend a digital food scale.

Seriously.

Initially, when weighing and measuring was first suggested to me, I refused to do it. And I kept struggling with my weight. But then I tried it, and what I found was that weighing my food with a digital scale actually gave me psychological freedom. When I weigh my food I know I'm getting the right amount. And when I hear that voice in my head telling me that maybe I didn't get enough food and I should have some more, I know it's lying to me and I can ignore it.

AUTOMATICITY—YOUR NEW BEST FRIEND

Bright Line Eating is carefully constructed so that eating behaviors are shifted out of the part of the brain where decisions are made, the prefrontal cortex, and into the part of the brain where things are automatic, the basal ganglia. Bright Line Eating takes some willpower to set up, of course, but uses little to no willpower at all after that.

We don't want you ever making *decisions* about what to eat next. When you're making decisions on the fly you are too vulnerable to the Willpower Gap and the voice of your Saboteur. We want to set you up so that all the crucial components of every Bright Line day are automatic. This accomplishes three goals: It takes the burden off of willpower, silences your internal food chatter, and, most important, keeps you at goal weight easily.

WHAT THIS LOOKS LIKE

The difference between using willpower and using your automatic brain to accomplish something is huge. If you've ever tried adding a new habit to your routine (jogging, getting the laundry going before work, meditation . . .), you've probably experienced what it's like to forget, get too busy, or decide to skip it. But now think about brushing your teeth. I bet in a year's time you will have accomplished brushing your teeth 730 times, regardless of travel, sickness, or work stress. It's non-negotiable. What's more, you spend exactly zero energy worrying that you won't get it done. When something becomes automatic, it frees up *tremendous* cognitive resources for other things.

Researchers have found that it takes, on average, 66 days for a behavior to become 95 percent automatic.[17] However, that was just an average and the range was immense. On the low end, automaticity was achieved in as few as 18 days, and on the high end, 254 days.

That means you're going to have to give yourself at least 18 to 254 days to focus on this pretty intensely. However, keep in mind that the people in that study were asked to add *one* new behavior to their life. Getting Happy, Thin, and Free is going to require adding several new behaviors, breaking many long-standing habits, and, for some, kicking an addiction too. That's a big ask.

BUNNY SLIPPERS

During the initial set-up period, before Bright Line Eating becomes automatic, I want you to be very protective of your willpower and do whatever you can not to overly deplete it. Reduce stress at work if possible. Bow out of that time-consuming committee. Be conscious of the activities that tap your resources, like moving your kids through their bedtime routine, and plan your Bright Line meals accordingly. Either eat dinner beforehand or have it laid out ready for you. Don't go straight from *Goodnight Moon* to the kitchen or you may end up in the Doritos.

In general, in the early days, I want you to imagine yourself going through your day wearing bunny slippers. Be kind to yourself. You may feel very tired for a few months. That's normal, and it will pass. Drink a lot of water and know that the fatigue is real, but it's temporary. The time for feeling fantastic and being out in the world is coming, but later. Right now, give yourself permission to be gentle with yourself. And a key part of that is . . .

NO EXERCISE

You were waiting for the good news? Yes, Bright Line Eating is a no-exercise plan. During the first four to five months of the weight-loss phase I strongly discourage people from starting a new exercise program because it depletes willpower, which is dangerous to your long-term goal. We have found in our Boot Camps that the people who insist on continuing to exercise lose the *least* amount

of weight. They're overtaxed. They can't keep their lines bright, and it all unravels from there.

Now, I am a huge believer in all the documented benefits of exercise and, as someone who has been Happy, Thin, and Free for more than a decade, I enjoy it tremendously. Once you've lost all your excess weight, or have been steady on the plan for months and the Bright Lines require no willpower from you, you'll probably find that you naturally want to get moving again.

It's also important to recognize that exercise is part of the pathology for many of us. Many of the regular exercisers who land in the Bright Line Eating Boot Camp have used overexercising to compensate for overeating for years. And they don't even realize it. But try to take it away from them, even for a few short months, even for a very good reason, and the neurosis starts to surface.

What we want at Bright Line Eating is to get to a place where exercise is valued for all its health benefits, but totally and completely uncoupled from weight loss in dieters' minds. They truly are not related.

AN INVITATION

If one or more of the things I said in the preceding sections shook you up, I understand. It's a big change from what you're used to. And . . . that's why it works. I invite you to just surrender to the plan. If you do it with full commitment, you will end up with a magical automaticity that will pay dividends for the rest of your life. Your efforts now will result in nearly every dream you've ever had for yourself coming true. And not just because you're thinner, but because you're *more you*, in every way. But if you don't carve out the time to do it right—if you insist on exercising too much, working too hard, and cutting corners—the system won't get set up properly; you'll hardwire in exceptions here and there, and this will go down in your history as one more thing that didn't work.

So, I invite you to decide right now to commit to the program as it's laid out—no wiggle room, no exceptions—and to *trust*. It's time to be unstoppable. It's time to give yourself the gift of really doing this.

CINDY RINAMAN MARSCH

Before

After

STARTING DATE February 16, 2017
HEAVIEST WEIGHT 292 pounds
STARTING WEIGHT 259 pounds
GOAL WEIGHT ACHIEVED April 29, 2018
CURRENT WEIGHT 180 pounds
HEIGHT 5'6"

I've always been a great cook, and mostly a healthy cook, and though I made a lot of foods that did not serve me well over the years, I mostly provided meals with lots of vegetables for my family. But in the worst seasons of my food prison it was store-bought things that fed my cravings, and I knew I was getting to a dark place when I eventually found myself doing that fast-food drive-in routine so many lament.

When I started BLE I immediately enjoyed the giant lunchtime salads with protein and fruit. I made great yogurt-based and tahini-based dressings and loved building a salad around a particular theme. Some Tex-Mex, some Italian, some salad Niçoise, and some based on flavorful cheeses or olives.

I keep a wipe-off board on my fridge for tallying up the ounces of veggies and beans and meat I use to make one of my favorite soups or chili or marinara, and I tweak final amounts to get good proportions that make a meal. Just about perfect is a soup where 2 cups contain a protein serving and 6 or 10 ounces of vegetables. I can measure this out into freezer containers, label it, and have an instant meal I can microwave in a pinch. It's like a gift I give myself!

Favorite flavor discoveries for other meals include grapefruit and banana, ground cloves on sweet potato or butternut squash, and a mixture of mayonnaise and mustard baked on top of fish. I had a hard time adjusting to the idea of eating yogurt without sweetener, but I found that just an ounce or two of banana mellows the tartness. A little banana also helps oatmeal carry tart berries. Fresh lemon zest or a grating of fresh ginger can do wonders for almost anything!

My options have expanded as I've moved into maintenance and I'm enjoying more choices in my menus. But the basics of our beautiful Bright Line foods are delightful in themselves—I can be perfectly content at an airport with a couple of salted boiled eggs and a collection of sugar snap peas, carrots, and fresh pepper strips with a piece of fresh fruit and nuts on the side.

I have had bright and shiny lines for two years and am confident I can fully enjoy eating this way for the rest of my life. The things I'm missing out on in my old life are totally not worth going back for. I look forward to new discoveries in healthy eating!

Chapter 2

How to Do
Bright Line Eating

*F*irst, I have to kick off this chapter by saying (and the experienced Bright Liner may have already noticed) that there is some overlap between the first book and this one—and that's especially true in this chapter. When it comes to what and how much to eat, there is also overlap between the Boot Camp and the books because these guidelines are relatively consistent and don't change much. So, if you are an experienced Bright Liner, you may at this point want to skip to Chapter 3, which offers the latest science behind how we chose these recipes and why they will work to get and keep you Happy, Thin, and Free. For everyone else, I will now present the essentials of what you need to know about the "eating" part of Bright Line Eating.

I want to start by reassuring you. There is an entire amazing world of food out there without sugar and flour. The foods you can eat on this plan are tremendously varied because Bright Line Eating is a *permanent* lifestyle. It's not about living on bars for six weeks . . . or grapefruit. It's about eating real food that is good for your brain in quantities that produce, and then sustain, your weight loss.

Okay, fair enough. Yet you still may be asking, "But will I *enjoy* it?"

Absolutely.

Eventually.

The first bit of good news: If downregulation was an issue for you, as your dopamine receptors heal you are going to find that you're able to taste your food in a way you may not have been able to for years. I say this as someone who gave up a pretty hard-core cookie-dough habit and now geeks out over how good my roasted vegetables taste. Second, every cell in your taste buds dies and is replaced by a brand-new taste bud cell *every two weeks*,[1] so as you detox, your taste buds will be going through their own evolution, and in very short order your food will taste delicious.

Third, you'll find that hunger has a huge impact on flavor. By coming to meals genuinely hungry—in other words, in need of your body's next dose of *fuel*, as opposed to its next hit of sugar and flour—what you'll find is that your food will actually taste better.[2] It turns out that true hunger has a huge impact on the way food tastes.

One warning: As you read through the food plan for the very first time, you may find yourself having a strong reaction to what seems like a complex, rigid, overwhelming system. That is very common. I promise it will get easy and feel simple very, very quickly.

It's kind of like becoming a new parent. On Day 1 a lot of new skills need to be mastered from a standstill; by Day 7 you could teach someone else how to do it, and by Day 30 you could write your own book.

Food is just complicated because there are so many options. I suggest you read this section through and then take some deep breaths and calm yourself down. Tell yourself to just try it for a while and see. No commitments, just see. Thousands of people have done this successfully, and there's no difference between them and you. This plan works beautifully if you follow it.

By "the plan" I am referring to the entire system of support that is Bright Line Eating. To reiterate, the food plan is just one component. This program isn't just about changing how you eat. Changing how you wake up, how you go to bed, how you interact with others, how you treat yourself, and how you think about life in between is what makes this program successful like nothing else.

Another point I repeat often: If you currently have a way of eating, like paleo, Nutritarian, vegan, or gluten-free, you can easily adapt this food plan to your needs and continue to adhere to the guidelines of that program. In 2012, I became an exclusively plant-based eater for about three years (now I'm *mostly* a plant-based eater), and Bright Line Eating has kept me beautifully slender, both for all the years that I included meat and dairy in my diet on a daily basis, and all the years since.

And finally, as you start to read this, I invite you to surrender and simply have an open mind. The most successful people in Bright Line Eating are those who decide to trust the full plan and do it as outlined. After all, nothing you've tried before has gotten you where you've wanted to be, right? Thousands of cases show that this road map works. Trust.

THE WEIGHT-LOSS FOOD PLAN

If you have at least 10 pounds to lose, this is where you'll start. You'll stay on this plan until you start to transition to goal weight. How long it will take you to reach that point, of course, depends on how much weight you have to lose and how quickly you lose. There is a wide range of how quickly people lose their excess weight doing Bright Line Eating, but on average people lose 1 to 3 pounds per week. It's important to note here that, contrary to widespread belief, there is actually no scientific evidence show-ing that it's better to lose weight slowly.[3] I say, get it off.

Also, I have seen again and again that people's goal weight shifts once they have seen their bodies respond to the plan. When I was struggling with my weight I was aim-ing to get down to a size 8. Size 4 was outside my realm of comprehension. That's all to say, set a goal, but don't be surprised if that number shifts down for you in a few months.

Once you're approaching goal weight I'll map out for you in the Maintenance Food Plan section all the details on how to transition your food plan to slow—then stop—your weight loss so you arrive gently in your right-sized body and then have the tools to stay there for the rest of your life.

BREAKFAST	1 protein
	1 breakfast grain
	1 fruit
LUNCH	1 protein
	6 oz. vegetables
	1 fruit
	1 fat
DINNER	1 protein
	6 oz. vegetables
	8 oz. salad
	1 fat

BREAKFAST GRAINS

Whole grains, like oats or brown rice, are perfectly fine on the Bright Line Eating plan, but at first you'll only have them at breakfast. When you're close to goal weight you'll add them to lunch, and then ultimately to dinner as well. True whole grains take 20 to 30 minutes (or even an hour or more, depending on the grain) to cook, so most people find that cooking them in bulk once or twice a week is the most convenient approach. We also count potatoes and sweet potatoes as "grains" in BLE and you'll see many wonderful sweet potato breakfast recipes in Chapter 4. Just cook them according to the recipe and measure out 4 ounces.

Many of us also eat instant or quick-cooking oatmeal. The two keys that make for a workable option are that it contains no sweeteners of any kind (including evaporated cane juice, artificial sweeteners, and the like) or any flour. Weigh out 1 ounce dry, add about 4 ounces of liquid, some salt to taste if you like, and microwave for 2 to 3 minutes.

For whole-grain cold cereal, weigh out exactly 1 ounce and either eat it dry (Shredded Wheat, for example, which has no flour, can be eaten dry, making it a good travel option) or add milk, unsweetened soymilk, or unsweetened yogurt (which you will count as your protein). Due to their extremely low protein and calorie contents, other non-dairy milks (such as almond) are not recommended during the weight-loss phase (unless you're splitting your protein serving in half; see the notes on breakfast proteins below).

PRECOOKED—Hot (weigh 4 oz. after cooking)	DRY—Cold or Hot (weigh 1 oz. dry, then cook)
Millet (4 oz. cooked)	Oat bran (1 oz. dry)
Potato (4 oz. cooked)	Oatmeal (1 oz. dry)
Quinoa (4 oz. cooked)	Commercial dry cereal* (1 oz.)
Rice (4 oz. cooked)	Cream of rice (1 oz. dry)
Sweet potato (4 oz. cooked)	Grits (1 oz. dry)
Yam (4 oz. cooked)	

* Sugar- and flour-free, commercially made, BLE-friendly dry cereals that people in our community have found include Uncle Sam's Original, Ezekiel Original, Fiber One Original, Shredded Wheat, and various plain puffed grain cereals (puffed rice, puffed wheat, etc.).

MAINTENANCE GRAINS

Once you are on Maintenance, which we will cover in depth below, you'll most likely be adding 4 or 6 ounces of grains to lunch and dinner as well. Here is a list of ones we like that you can also use for maintenance breakfasts if you enjoy them:

Amaranth Potatoes	Kamut	Rye	Triticale
Barley	Kaniwa	Sorghum	Wheat
Buckwheat	Millet	Spelt	Wild rice
Bulgur	Quinoa	Sweet potatoes	Yams
Farro	Rice (any kind)	Teff	

PROTEINS

For breakfast proteins, yogurt is an excellent choice, and regular and Greek yogurt are equally suitable. The preference would be for low-fat rather than non-fat or whole-milk products, but there's no hard-and-fast rule on this. Seeds are also wonderful. Nuts and especially nut butters are only a good idea if they aren't a binge food for you; also keep in mind that they are calorically very dense, so include no more than two servings a week until you've lost all your weight.

If you prefer plant-based proteins, it is best to avoid almond milk, hemp milk, flax milk, or rice milk for your breakfast protein during the weight-loss phase because the unsweetened versions are very light on both calories and protein and they won't hold you until lunch. Fortified soy milk is a better choice.

However, if you very much want to have, say, almond milk for breakfast, here's a way to make that work. Split your protein serving in half, and have 4 ounces of any kind of milk and 1 ounce of nuts or seeds (or half a serving of cheese, eggs, or any other protein you like). The benefit of, in particular, the almond/soy milk + nuts/seeds combination is that one is a little too light and one is a little too heavy, so they balance each other out perfectly. You can split your breakfast protein like this every day if you like. I do.

An important tip on lunch and dinner proteins: You always want to weigh your food *after* you cook it. For example, if you're going to eat a hamburger, don't weigh out your hamburger patty and then put it on the grill or in the frying pan; it will shrink down by a whopping 25 to 50 percent. So when you cook food, including proteins and vegetables, cook enough for several servings of leftovers, and weigh out your immediate serving after it's fully cooked.

Bacon is not on the food plan for one main reason: 4 to 6 ounces of bacon is just a heckuva lot of bacon. But if you're traveling and eating breakfast at a buffet, splitting your protein and having a couple of strips of bacon with scrambled eggs would make sense. But note: Be *very* careful about processed meats like bacon, lunch meats, hot dogs, or sausage. You need to read the ingredients list carefully and make sure that sugar (such as dextrose), flour, or some kind of starch aren't in the first three ingredients on the list. They're also unhealthy, so if you can avoid them and eat real meats, ideally organic, compassionately raised meats, you're much better off.

For plant-based protein, tempeh that's made out of soy and some kind of grain (like brown rice) is fine. Smoky tempeh strips are very tasty and also a good choice. Beans and lentils are some of your least expensive and most healthy protein and fiber options, so include them often. Soy nuts are great to keep in a little preweighed baggie in your purse, briefcase, or travel bag if you choose to eat plant-based, so you have a ready protein option with you wherever you go. You can discreetly dump them onto your salad in a restaurant to round out a meal. They're not listed, but dried or roasted beans (like chickpeas) are also wonderful and can be included with the same weight measurement as soy nuts (2 ounces for women;

3 ounces for men). I've found little snack baggies of dried chickpeas in airport gift shops and enjoyed them for breakfast with fresh fruit and some Starbucks oatmeal after a red-eye flight.

It is important to note that not all plant-based cheeses are Bright Line friendly. Some contain quite a bit of flour or tapioca starch. You must check your ingredient list and make sure that, like salad dressing, the cheese does not have a refined carbohydrate in the first three ingredients.

ANIMAL-BASED PROTEINS Typically Eaten at Breakfast (WOMEN)	ANIMAL-BASED PROTEINS Typically Eaten at Lunch/Dinner (WOMEN)	ANIMAL-BASED PROTEINS Typically Eaten at Breakfast (MEN)	ANIMAL-BASED PROTEINS Typically Eaten at Lunch/Dinner (MEN)
8 oz. plain yogurt	4 oz. chicken (not breaded, skin off)	8 oz. plain yogurt	6 oz. chicken (not breaded, skin off)
8 oz. milk	4 oz. turkey (skin off)	8 oz. milk	6 oz. turkey (skin off)
2 eggs	4 oz. pork (not bacon, no ham cured in sugar)	3 eggs	6 oz. pork (not bacon, no ham cured in sugar)
2 oz. cheese	4 oz. beef (ground beef, steak, sirloin tips, etc.)	3 oz. cheese	6 oz. beef (ground beef, steak, sirloin tips, etc.)
4 oz. cottage cheese	4 oz. lamb	6 oz. cottage cheese	6 oz. lamb
4 oz. ricotta cheese	4 oz. fish	6 oz. ricotta cheese	6 oz. fish
	4 oz. shrimp or other shellfish		6 oz. shrimp or other shellfish

PLANT-BASED PROTEINS Typically Eaten at Breakfast (WOMEN)	PLANT-BASED PROTEINS Typically Eaten at Lunch/Dinner (WOMEN)	PLANT-BASED PROTEINS Typically Eaten at Breakfast (MEN)	PLANT-BASED PROTEINS Typically Eaten at Lunch/Dinner (MEN)
8 oz. unsweetened soy milk	4 oz. tofu	8 oz. unsweetened soy milk	6 oz. tofu
8 oz. unsweetened almond milk	4 oz. tempeh	8 oz. unsweetened almond milk	6 oz. tempeh
8 oz. unsweetened other nondairy milk (hemp, flax, rice, etc.)	6 oz. beans (or 2 oz. roasted beans, like roasted chickpeas)	8 oz. unsweetened other nondairy milk (hemp, flax, rice, etc.)	6 oz. beans (or 3 oz. roasted beans, like roasted chickpeas)
4 oz. tofu	6 oz. lentils	6 oz. tofu	6 oz. lentils
4 oz. hummus	4 oz. hummus	6 oz. hummus	6 oz. hummus
2 oz. soya granules	4 oz. shelled edamame	3 oz. soya granules	6 oz. shelled edamame
2 oz. nuts (or nut butters)	4 oz. veggie burger	2 oz. nuts (or nut butters)	6 oz. veggie burger
2 oz. seeds	2 oz. soy nuts (or dry-roasted edamame)	2 oz. seeds	3 oz. soy nuts (or dry-roasted edamame)

FRUIT

If the size of the fruit is unusual, you can always fall back on your trusty scale and weigh 6 ounces. For example, some bananas are very small, and you may want to weigh 6 ounces of banana. Some plums and apricots are huge, and you may want to weigh 6 ounces, rather than having two or three pieces. For cherries, you can weigh your 6 ounces with the pits still in and not worry about the weight of the pits, or you can weigh 6.3 ounces with the pits in (or 6¼ ounces if your scale uses fractions—yes, I once carefully removed and then weighed the pits in 6 ounces of cherries), or you can use a cherry pitter and remove the pits before weighing the cherries.

HAVE 1 PIECE	HAVE 2 PIECES	HAVE 3 PIECES	WEIGH 6 OUNCES
Apple	Kiwi	Apricot	Berries (all kinds)
Banana	Persimmon		Cherries
Grapefruit	Plum		Fresh figs
Nectarine			Grapes
Orange			Mango/papaya
Peach			Melon (all kinds)
Pear			Pineapple

VEGETABLES

You can prepare your vegetables raw or cooked, serve them as a salad, or have some combination thereof. Chapter 5 will tell you how to prepare, store, and enjoy vegetables. Here I'll just say we have a saying in Bright Line Eating: "Produce is produce." This means that if you don't feel like eating a salad at dinner, you can have cooked vegetables instead. Be sure to weigh your vegetables *after* you cook them, because, just like protein, the veggies will shrink, sometimes dramatically, in the cooking process.

When it comes to cooking vegetables in oil, people have various approaches, all of which you will see in the recipes later in the book. Some people only steam their vegetables, or use nonstick pans to avoid using any of their fat serving in the process. Others measure out their olive or coconut oil and count that as their fat serving. Still others just use a light, quick mist of olive oil spray and don't count it at all, which is fine. What we want to avoid is doing something like cooking collard greens in butter and ham hocks. Vegetables are not to be used as a saturated fat delivery mechanism.

Canned or frozen vegetables are fine, but be sure there's nothing added to them. For example, canned beets are delicious, but you have to find ones packed in water with no added sugar; similarly, find artichoke hearts packed in water, not oil. Some frozen vegetables come in a buttery sauce or have added sugar—avoid these. For corn you can measure out 6 ounces of corn kernels or you can have two small ears or one large ear of fresh corn on the cob.

Starchy vegetables are fine to count as vegetables, but be aware that their calorie count is relatively high compared to other vegetables. For this reason I recommend that you limit your starchy vegetables to two servings a week during the weight-loss phase. After you've lost your weight you can experiment with eating them more often, so long as your weight stays stable.

Notice that potatoes, sweet potatoes, and yams are not on the list of starchy vegetables. They all count as grains, and you'll be eating them again at lunch and dinner when you're at goal weight.

And please don't make the mistake of thinking that 8 ounces of salad means 8 ounces of lettuce. You'd be chewing all night! You'll want to start off with a base of about 2 to 3 ounces of a heavy lettuce, like romaine or iceberg, or 1 to 2 ounces of a lighter lettuce, like baby spinach or spring mix. Then add crunchy salad vegetables like tomatoes, cucumbers, carrots, red onion, mushrooms, peppers, sprouts, jicama, beets, celery, etc. on top of that until the total weight equals exactly 8 ounces. After you reach goal weight, if it doesn't cause your weight to creep up, you can add some avocado or olives as vegetables, but during the weight-loss phase it's best to avoid these, as they are calorically very dense and high in fat. In fact, you'll notice that they're listed as fats in the BLE plan. When eating out, be sure to order your salad carefully so that it comes with only vegetables and no croutons, cheese, dried fruit, fresh fruit, bacon bits, or heavy dressing. Ask for olive oil and vinegar on the side. You can use a spoon to measure out your oil: 3 teaspoons equals 1 tablespoon. Then add vinegar to taste.

Variety is especially important when it comes to vegetables. If you're not familiar with many of the vegetables listed here, try to incorporate a new one from the vegetables section of this cookbook every week until your repertoire is greatly expanded. Variety is not only the spice of life, it is the cornerstone of health and vitality!

VEGETABLES

Artichoke hearts	Asparagus	Beet greens	Beets
Broccoli	Broccoli rabe	Brussels sprouts	Cabbage
Carrots	Celery	Collard greens	Cucumber
Eggplant	Garlic	Green beans	Kale
Lettuce	Mushrooms	Onions	Peppers
Radishes	Snow peas	Spaghetti squash	Spinach
Swiss chard	Tomatillo	Tomatoes	Turnip greens
Yellow (summer) squash	Zucchini		

STARCHY VEGETABLES
(Acceptable but use sparingly)

Corn	Turnip/rutabaga/swede	Parsnips	Winter squash (butternut, delicata, acorn, pumpkin)

FATS

You'll add one serving of fat to your food at both lunch and dinner. For lunch, perhaps you'll choose to put the fat on your vegetables. For dinner, I suspect you'll want to add oil or dressing to your salad. You can use a tablespoon measure for your fat, but I personally prefer to weigh it on my digital food scale because it's less messy and more precise. If you're going to weigh it, 1 tablespoon equals ½ ounce (or 0.5 ounces) on the scale. Be careful, though—if you're weighing oil and it goes over, you have to be prepared to grab a paper towel and sop some up to get it back down to the correct weight. You never want to get sloppy with the scale. Don't succumb to the Saboteur who whispers in your ear and says, "It's only a tiny bit—it doesn't matter." It *does* matter. It's a matter of integrity. It's your Bright Line.

In terms of fat, you want to keep in mind that there's a huge difference to your body between healthier fats, like almonds and avocados, and unhealthy fats, like soybean oil or vegetable oil, especially if they're partially hydrogenated. Vegetable oil of some kind is what you'll find in most bottled salad dressings and mayonnaise.[4] If you're going to be heating up your food, then olive oil, coconut oil, or canola oil are good choices. If you're going to be putting oil on a salad, I suggest using flax oil. It's a wonderful source of omega-3 fatty acids, which most of us are desperately lacking in our diet. You can't heat up flax oil, though, or it will denature the molecules due to its low smoke point. If you like to add butter to your food, that's fine, but if you prefer to be plant-based, there are many excellent butter substitutes. If you're going to use a bottled salad dressing, see if you can find one that uses olive oil instead of soybean or vegetable oil. The biggest red flag about bottled salad dressings is that they almost all contain some sugar or other type of sweetener. If the sweetener is very far down on the ingredients list—fourth or lower—then it's okay. It won't be sweet enough to trigger cravings. Just make sure that no sweeteners are listed in the first three ingredients on the list. Clearly a raspberry vinaigrette or honey-mustard dressing won't work—it will most definitely have a sweetener (maybe two) in the first three ingredients.

Ranch dressings vary; some are okay and some have sugar in the first three ingredients. Most blue cheese dressings will work and many, but not all, vinaigrette dressings will work. Just make it a habit to read the ingredients list.

FATS	
Avocado (2 oz.)	Butter (1 tablespoon or 0.5 oz.)
Cheese (1 oz.)	Hummus (2 oz.)
Margarine (1 tablespoon or 0.5 oz.)	Mayonnaise (1 tablespoon or 0.5 oz.)
Nut butter (1 tablespoon or 0.5 oz.)	Nuts (0.5 oz.)
Olives (2 oz.)	Oil (1 tablespoon or 0.5 oz.)
Salad dressing (1 tablespoon or 0.5 oz.)	Seeds (0.5 oz.)
Tahini (1 tablespoon or 0.5 oz.)	

CONDIMENTS

CONDIMENTS	
Capers (2 oz. per meal)	Mustard
Cinnamon	Nutritional yeast (0.5 oz. per meal)
Herbs	Salsa (2 oz. per meal)
Hot sauce	Salt and pepper
Lemon juice	Soy sauce
Lime juice	Spices
Marinara sauce (2 oz. per meal)	Vinegar (including balsamic)

Bright Line Eating is a program of clear boundaries, not asceticism or deprivation. I absolutely think our food should be delicious, and we should enjoy it heartily. But after it's over, it's back to life. Condiments, spices, herbs, and salt and pepper are simple and easy additions that can make a meal fabulous. Just make sure there's no sugar or flour in the first three ingredients. Always read the ingredients list. And keep an eye on your use—I have known people (including myself) to go overboard on salsa, nutritional yeast, cinnamon, mustard, and balsamic vinegar, among others—and when I notice myself falling into this pattern I tend to just let that particular condiment go for a while.

A word about salt. Sodium and chloride ions play important roles in cellular processes, including synaptic transmission in the brain. When you stop eating the Standard American Diet and give up packaged foods in favor of whole, real foods, your sodium intake is going to drop precipitously. If you have very high blood pressure, that's a good thing. If your blood pressure is low or normal, though, you might start to feel dizzy sometimes. This can often be alleviated by drinking plenty of water and consuming a bit more salt. Contrary to popular belief, research shows that not getting enough salt can have serious health consequences.[5] Unless you have high blood pressure, you may want to start salting your food on the Bright Line Eating food plan. Seriously. Of course, talk with your doctor about this.

BEVERAGES AND ALCOHOL

What can you drink with Bright Line Eating? Let me tell you what I drink: I drink water. When I'm at a party or restaurant, I drink sparkling water with lemon or lime. It's fine to squeeze the lemon or lime in there as long as you're not eating the whole thing, because that's a snack. Also, the sparkling waters that have natural flavors infused in them—but don't have artificial sweeteners—are fine. I also drink herbal teas of all varieties. I particularly like peppermint, ginger, and India-spiced chai, but it seems I'm discovering a delightful new blend regularly.

Beverages that I'm not so thrilled about are coffee, caffeinated tea, and alcohol, but they're not equal offenders.

Coffee and Tea. Unsweetened herbal teas of all kinds are a wonderful boon to the Bright Line way of life. Enjoy them freely. Many Bright Lifers have found that making a soothing cup of herbal tea can really save the day. Black, decaffeinated coffee is also fine and can be a wonderful addition to your morning or a postrestaurant meal conversation.

Now the nuanced topic: caffeine. Since writing *Bright Line Eating*, my thoughts on caffeine have evolved based on the data we have been getting from our Bright Lifers. It turns out that caffeine response falls on a continuum, just like addictive susceptibility, but there seems to be no direct correlation between the two. For example, I am a 10++ on the Susceptibility Scale, but my caffeine response falls in the middle. On the low end of the scale are people who have kept their lines bright and shiny for years, living happily at goal weight, and coffee is an integral part of their day. It has no ill effects for them and does not lead to cravings or line breakage. In the middle are people like me: Caffeine doesn't interfere with my Bright Lines, but it does make my daily meditation less satisfying and also allows me to override very real fatigue, leading to burnout. For that reason I try to abstain. (Although, I have been experimenting with two daily servings of strong matcha green tea because of its many health benefits and it's going well so far. But it's still an experiment.) Then, on the high end of the spectrum are people for whom coffee is always a gateway drug. It leads to food thoughts, cravings, and line breakage.

You won't know where you are on the caffeine continuum until you run the experiment. As you do, note that if you are someone for whom sugar grazing has been an issue, you may have been in a cycle of using caffeine to recover from insulin crashes. You may find that once you eliminate sugar from your diet your energy levels stabilize naturally and your need for caffeine gradually disappears.

Lastly I have to mention that our commercial food culture has conflated caffeine with sugar. Most beverages for sale at American coffee chains are loaded with sugar. Or people order unsweetened drinks, and then add four or five packets of artificial sweetener. This is why, for many people, just the taste of coffee brings back powerful sugar cravings.

So here is my recommendation: For the first few months of your weight-loss journey, try abstaining. Then, once you have all your good habits firmly in place, be a scientist. See where you fall on the spectrum. Take a breath and be aware. We live in a culture that mindlessly chugs coffee. I invite you to slow down and see what your brain's true relationship to it is.

Alcohol. Let's talk about alcohol. Molecularly, alcohol is sugar plus ethanol. Ethanol makes you intoxicated. So basically, alcohol is sugar that lowers your resistance to doing foolish things and making choices you wouldn't otherwise make. Anytime you drink alcohol, you're going to be more likely to eat something that's off your food plan. So alcohol is off the Bright Line Eating plan because it's sugar, and doubly so because it makes you intoxicated and reduces your inhibitions.

Now, that said, I have to admit that I do know a couple of people who are in the midrange on the Susceptibility Scale (a 6 or below) who succeed at Bright Line Eating and have found that they can incorporate one serving of red wine once in a while at a special occasion. I have personally never seen alcohol work for anyone who is above a 6 on the scale. But I have seen it drive a lot of people crazy. Most Bright Lifers have found that in order to live Happy, Thin, and Free, they need to classify alcohol as sugar and maintain a firm Bright Line. Of course, I never deny anyone their research.

GETTING STARTED

1. Visit Your Doctor

This is the step that many people, in their understandable eagerness to get started, want to skip. I *highly* encourage you not to. First, if you are currently on any medications for medical conditions, it's very important to have your doctor's support and involvement. One thing I've seen over and over is that people's medications often need to be adjusted very quickly on this plan. Make an action plan for how frequently you should check back in for potential adjustments.

Second, you want to get a full blood workup: cholesterol panel, A1C, triglycerides, blood pressure, fasting blood glucose, baseline insulin reading, and any other numbers that you and your doctor want to track. Things are about to change for you, rapidly and dramatically, and you can never get back that window into what your body was like at the beginning.

2. Take Your "Before" Pictures

Some people do this with eagerness and joy. For others, it's torture. You do not need to be in a bikini—leggings or shorts and a tank top will do just fine. You may be tempted to wear black, but bright colors are better. You also don't have to show anyone your pictures—just *take* them. If you have resistance, please trust me on this one. Starting Bright Line Eating and not taking pictures of your "before" state is like raising a child and never taking baby pictures. You'll never get this back. And this will work. No one will believe that you were ever fat, and you won't have proof. I am speaking from experience here. At one point in my journey I was a size 24. My best fat picture shows me at a size 16. Don't make that mistake. Please.

3. Clean Out Your Kitchen

Donate, give away, or throw away everything that's not on your food plan. Check the refrigerator door for dressings, sauces, and condiments and clear out everything that has sugar or any sweetener listed in the first three ingredients.

If you live with others, clear out as much as you can, while keeping things that your family or roommates eat. I have three young girls, so we still have plenty of foods that I don't eat in my house. Depending on your circumstances, consider carving out a refrigerator shelf and kitchen cupboard that will be only for your food. Or vice versa. Create a low or high shelf for their food. Perhaps pack all their snacks or sweets in a drawer or cupboard that you can simply avoid. However you do it, arrange your space to minimize triggers.

4. Things to Buy

A. Digital food scale. You don't need a fancy one with a calorie counter, nutrition information, or printer—just a plain old food scale is all you need. But it must be digital. You don't want the ambiguity of trying to decide whether the needle is on the line, and you *definitely* don't want to be obsessing about how much lettuce you can smoosh into a measuring cup.

B. Travel containers for food. Unless I am flying, I use glass or Pyrex containers to store and reheat my food. Yes, they are heavier in my lunch tote, but they have no chemicals that have been shown to interfere with weight loss. If you want to keep something especially hot or cold, consider a thermal lunch bag as well.

C. Food journal. You could also use an app (Bright Line Eating is developing new technologies all the time; check ble.life/cookbook for the latest), a note page on your smartphone, or post your food online, but at the very minimum have it written in a journal. Keep it by your fridge in your kitchen with a pen.

D. Gratitude journal. Keep this by your bed to write in before you go to sleep. Again, I suggest making it something you visually enjoy having by you. If you're crafty, decorating the front cover can be a fun project. Post the picture of your handiwork in our Online Support Community!

E. Bathroom scale. You'll want to make sure you have a good digital bathroom scale. An analog scale with a needle and an arc of numbers simply isn't a good choice these days. Toss it out and go get yourself a digital bathroom scale. You'll want one that weighs in half-pound—or perhaps even smaller—increments.

DAY 1: ANATOMY OF A SUCCESSFUL DAY

Your success on Day 1 is going to depend heavily on your preparations the evening before. Here's your mini-checklist:

→ Look in your fridge and decide what you're going to eat the next day.

→ Pick up your food journal by the fridge and write "Day 1" at the top of the first page.

→ Write the next day's date.

→ Write down what you are committing to eat the next day.

→ Then get a good night's sleep. You are about to be rocketed into the fourth dimension.

In the morning on Day 1, you'll want to get your starting weight. Always weigh yourself first thing in the morning, naked, immediately after using the restroom. Some people weigh daily, some weekly, some monthly, depending on what they find supports the right ratio of staying encouraged while keeping the agita at bay. I am a huge fan of weekly, because it means you won't go too far off course if things need to be fine-tuned, and you also won't read too much into the natural daily fluctuations. Daily can make you crazy, but some people just love it.

For the rest of your day, consider whether you'll need to pack and bring any of your meals with you. Better safe than sorry: If there's even the remote possibility that you may be out, bring your food. Remember silverware, a napkin, a sharp knife to cut your fruit if necessary, salt and pepper, and a nice big bottle of water.

Today you'll focus on eating your precommitted three meals and nothing in between. Weigh your food precisely. No BLTs—bites, licks, or tastes—while you're cooking, which means no popping veggies into your mouth off the cutting board. Your first bite of food should be after you're sitting at the table and have taken a couple of deep breaths. Reflect for a moment on how good it feels to keep your commitment to yourself and eat exactly what you planned to eat. The purpose of this kind of precision is that you're building up integrity and credibility with *yourself*.

THE TOOLS THAT MAKE IT WORK

In my first book, *Bright Line Eating*, I go into great detail about the rituals and support that help you stay on track, committed, and successful. Here are a few of them, but, again, I highly encourage you to make sure you are getting the full complement of resources, either from the first book or from joining the online Boot Camp.

COMMITTING YOUR FOOD

Committing your food is one of the key components of Bright Line Eating that takes the load off of willpower. Many studies have verified that a verbal or public commitment of some specific action that you're going to take is an incredibly effective way to bolster willpower and increase success.[6] It works, and it's an invaluable habit to build.

You can do it in the evening, right after you write down your food for the next day, or you can do it the following morning before the day starts. Whichever you pick, always do it the same way consistently. Again, we're building *habits* to take the load off of willpower.

→ One of the options is to commit your food in writing in the Bright Line Eating Online Support Community. If you're in the Bright Line Eating Boot Camp, you'll notice a lot of people doing this. You type in exactly what you're going to eat and then write, "Here's my food commitment for tomorrow. I commit to eating only and exactly that." One of the benefits of committing your food in the Online Support Community is that it's not going to miss your phone call. It's not going to leave the program. It's there for you in perpetuity. So you can rely on it, always, as a platform for committing your food.

→ The second way is to commit your food live on the phone to another human being. The benefit of this method is that you know there's a specific individual who holds the commitment for you, and you will be accountable to tell them the next day that you stuck to your commitment. It's very powerful.

→ The third way is more private: committing your food to yourself or your Higher Power and having a ritual around how you do that. It's simple, portable, and efficient. The downside is that it's less public, and research shows[7] that committing things publicly, either to another human being or to a community forum, like our Online Support Community, is really, really effective.

Writing down your food in advance is the foundation of the BLE program. Committing it takes that action to a much higher level. I encourage you to choose the way that works best for you and stick to it. Consistency is key.

BREAKING OUR BRIGHT LINES

In Bright Line Eating, we celebrate the strength in our shared commitment to sticking with the Bright Lines, a commitment to no exceptions, to being unstoppable. This gives us the physical recovery we're seeking—lasting weight loss and brilliant health—and it also results in a lot of freedom and happiness. This is what's so counterintuitive for people who don't need Bright Line Eating. Having clear structure can lead to so much freedom.

However, we also work on having a gentle, wise, and self-supportive approach when we do break our Bright Lines. Not everyone who embarks on this way of life will have breaks—some grab hold of this program like a lifeline and just follow the plan, one day at a time, indefinitely. Others deviate, either on purpose or under duress, and then work to get back on track. I myself have not had unbroken Bright Lines since I first started eating this way on May 21, 2003. I've had long stretches of shiny Bright Lines (as long as eight consecutive years) and other periods when I was struggling mightily to keep my Lines bright. Through that experience, I came to realize that there are four key components to handling a break in the Bright Lines successfully, adaptively, and in a way that strengthens our program. They are the Four S's.

1. SPEED

After veering off their diet, people often say they're going to "resume"—tomorrow, on Monday, after the holidays, or after their vacation. In Bright Line Eating we don't delay. We don't resume, we *rezoom*. With our very next meal, we get back on track. Because you don't want to fall prey to the "what-the-hell effect." This is a technical term in the psychology of eating literature[8] for the mental phenomenon that happens in chronic dieters when they think, *I've had one bite of pizza; I might as well eat the whole pizza and a half gallon of ice cream while I'm at it. I'll start my diet again later.*

No. Let's go. Like, now. Not tomorrow morning. Not on Monday. Not on January 1, but now.

2. SELF-COMPASSION

Inside your head, treat yourself like you'd treat your best friend who just sprained her ankle on a hike. You'd get her help. Rally resources. Make sure she was resting and taking it easy. No downward, negative spiral of self-loathing. Because shame over eating leads to more overeating. Be gentle, kind, and encouraging. You are not a bad person. You just have a malfunctioning brain.

3. SOCIAL SUPPORT

In my experience, the first thing that comes up after a break is a profound desire to *isolate*. But shame flourishes in silence. The most effective thing to do when you've had a break is to reach out to other people who do Bright Line Eating and who are walking this journey with you. Let them help you construct your plan for rezooming. They can probably see what you need much better than you can at the moment.

4. SEEK THE LESSON

After every break you should absolutely take an inventory of your life, your thinking, and your behavior leading up to the first bite. Odds are, you're not using the tools fully. Are you overly busy? Not letting yourself rest? Putting off meditation?

Not using your Nightly Checklist Sheet (a tool included with my first book, as well as the Boot Camp)? Or is it something else, like you can't stand to say no to other people's food offerings in social situations? Whatever it is, it's a growth opportunity. Get curious.

I want to end by saying that there's a continuum of sticking with the Bright Lines. There's sticking with the Bright Lines perfectly from Day 1, which I relate to, celebrate, and honor, because that's my story with my Bright Lines for drugs and alcohol from the moment I got clean and sober at 20 years old. And then, on the other end of that continuum, there's struggle and barely being able to string two days together of Bright Line Eating, and I relate to that, too. When I was living in Sydney, Australia, and went from a size 4 to a size 24 in three months, I was doing everything in my power to stop eating and I *just couldn't* until the tsunami of food addiction receded. It took what it took.

If you are doing Bright Line Eating and it's going well, *protect that*. Your Saboteur, I guarantee, will try to convince you to make an exception here or there. *Don't fall for it*. That road is slippery and painful. The fact that rezooming is possible is *absolutely not* an invitation to take a slight detour from the Lines and then get back on track right afterward. It doesn't work like that. The first thing that happens when you break the Bright Lines is that your freedom evaporates, instantly. And it goes downhill from there. You don't want to live a life of breaking and rezooming. The reason we honor the Bright Lines and commit to living within them is because we find that it makes us Happy, Thin, and Free. But more than that, it allows us to be more of the people we strive to be and to do more of the things we want to do in life beyond food—to be self-actualized and engaged in the world. *That* is what we want our lives to be about.

GETTING TO GOAL WEIGHT

Two important things about getting to goal weight. First, unlike with other diets, goal weight is not a destination you arrive at and then you stop doing Bright Line Eating. That's a prescription for regaining all your weight, yet again. Bright Line Eating is an identity—a way of life. It's not the kind of thing you do temporarily and then stop. I have been eating like this since 2003 and I have been a size 4 since I got to goal weight in 2004.

Second, there is a balance, once you reach maintenance, between getting too thin, which we don't want you to do, and regaining weight, which we don't want either. So we find the right quantities of protein, vegetables, fruits, fats, and whole grains that are exactly what your body needs to function optimally each day—no more, no less. But for each person that equation will be slightly different. What follows are general guidelines, but you will tweak this to find the perfect balance where you are neither gaining nor losing weight and you are maintaining mental food freedom.

The key is to *gradually* add more food to your plan until your weight loss stops and you are exactly at the weight you want to be.

Once you are 10 pounds from your goal weight you need to be weighing yourself at least weekly. Monthly weighing isn't frequent enough to give you the data you need. Daily is fine too, but for this transition process it's the weekly numbers you want to focus on.

The key factor determining your next step: On average, how fast are you losing your weight? The options are Super-Fast, Fast, Medium, or Slow. Super-Fast is 2.5 to 3 pounds (or more) per week. More often than not, it's men who are in that category. Fast is 2 pounds per week, on average. Medium is 1.5 pounds per week, and Slow is 1 pound or less per week. If your weight loss has slowed down over time, use your current rate of weight loss.

HOW TO TRANSITION TO MAINTENANCE

START HERE with the Weight-Loss Food Plan

1.	Add 4 oz. cooked grain to lunch.
2.	Increase breakfast grain to 1½ servings.
3.	Add 1 protein serving to breakfast.
4.	Add 4 oz. cooked grain to dinner.

THIS IS A TYPICAL FEMALE MAINTENANCE FOOD PLAN

5.	Add 1 fruit to dinner.
6.	Increase lunch grain to 6 oz.
7.	Increase dinner grain to 6 oz.
8.	Increase breakfast grain to 2 servings.

THIS IS A TYPICAL MALE MAINTENANCE FOOD PLAN

9.	Increase lunch vegetables to 8 oz.
10.	Increase dinner fat to 2 servings.
11.	Increase lunch fat to 2 servings.
12.	Increase lunch grain to 8 oz.
13.	Increase dinner grain to 8 oz.
14.	Add 1 oz. nuts to breakfast.
15.	Add 1 oz. nuts to lunch.
16.	Add 1 oz. nuts to dinner.

Some athletes and exceptionally active individuals eat this much or more!

ADDING BACK FOOD

Here's what to expect, based on my years of experience helping thousands of people.

1. It may scare you. You have been so committed for so long to eating a certain way that adding food may feel downright wrong. It might be super uncomfortable. You may feel resistance to going through with it. But at this transition point, adding in food is making a *healthy* choice for yourself. So lean in to the Online Support Community or your personal support group and breathe through it.

2. You'll be terrified of gaining your weight back. This is also a completely natural response to changing things up after months of watching the weight pour off you. As long as you continue to stick to your Bright Lines, that won't happen. You won't regain your lost weight.

3. Your weight may indeed pop up right away when you add food. THIS IS NORMAL. Keep that food in, and continue to be precise with your weighing and measuring. Within a week or two (if not sooner), your weight should come right back down to where it was. Then, after your body has stabilized with the additional food, you should start to lose weight again. That's when you add the next thing. Keep watching. If, a week later, you're still losing weight, add more food. If not, wait and watch. Again, it's a process.

The most important thing is to take the transition to maintenance seriously. Pour as much effort and energy into it as you did when you started Bright Line Eating in the first place. This will be hard to do, because you won't have that eager beginner's motivation. But mastering the maintenance dance requires learning an entirely new set of skills, and it takes focused attention and lots of support to do it successfully. My recommendation is to be in Bright Lifers and benefit from the myriad maintenance tools and targeted coaching that are available there. It's heartbreaking to

watch someone learn the Bright Line Eating system, follow it faithfully, reach goal weight, and then have it all unravel because they distanced themselves from the Mothership and didn't trust that the same source of guidance that helped them get the weight off would help them learn to keep it off, too.

SLOW WEIGHT LOSS

You have it the easiest. Stay on the Weight-Loss Food Plan until you are *at your* goal weight. Then add one bit of food. The table says the first thing to add is 4 ounces of grain at lunch, but if you're typically hungrier before lunch than you are before dinner, you may choose to increase your breakfast first. In this case add #2 and then #3 to get your breakfast up to your Maintenance level. Remember to keep in mind what I said—that your weight may pop up a bit. Just hold steady.

Some people do stay on the Weight-Loss Food Plan indefinitely because it's the right amount of food for their body. But if you've been losing weight and you're getting down to goal weight, that's probably not you. You're probably going to need to add at least something to stabilize.

MEDIUM WEIGHT LOSS

Add your first food (either to lunch or breakfast, see above) when you've got about 2 to 3 pounds to go before goal weight. Then follow the steps above. When you add something and just don't lose any more weight, you've found your maintenance plan.

FAST AND SUPER-FAST WEIGHT LOSS

Add your first food when you're 5 pounds from goal weight. If your weight loss is Super-Fast, add your first food when you're 10 pounds from goal weight. Then follow the steps above.

Note that for many, if not most, people, goal weight is a bit of a moving target, and maintenance is like a dance. Odds are, you're not going to settle on one food plan and stick with it forever. Bodies change, metabolisms change, notions of what goal weight is change, and you may need to add or take away food accordingly. Weighing yourself at least weekly during maintenance is recommended. You'll want and need that data to inform your journey.

DENISE FITZSIMMONS

Before

After

STARTING DATE **September 27, 2017**
HEAVIEST WEIGHT **208 pounds**
STARTING WEIGHT **178 pounds**
GOAL WEIGHT ACHIEVED **June 16, 2018**
CURRENT WEIGHT **123 pounds**
HEIGHT **5'7"**

*P*rior to BLE, my life centered on what the next meal would be and how exciting it would taste. I didn't binge, but I grazed continually. My food served as a comfort in all the ups and downs of life, but my focus on food kept me from realizing how sad I really was and also the fact that I had a spending addiction—none of which I would confront until I got my food clean.

During the weight-loss phase, the focus was on planning and absorbing everything I could about the science. I needed to know why I did this to myself. My Lines were not perfect, but I learned to rezoom really well. I was fortunate to lose the weight relatively quickly, and at the advice of my doctor I chose the goal of 125 pounds. I am totally happy as a size 4.

I jumped into Bright Lifers with the last available credits on my credit card because I was determined not to stop midway. The bonds I have created through the Online Support Community have been lifesaving. I learned along the way that the plan's benefit is much more than weight loss. My body just plain feels better. And now, when I break my Lines, I can feel how truly toxic sugar and flour are for me.

I do continue to eat animal protein, but only at one meal a day, which helps me control my food budget better. I also enjoy discovering new fruits and vegetables. Jackfruit and chayote are my new loves.

The transformation inside and out can best be compared to the sun breaking through after a good hard rain. These days, my relationships—family, friends, pets, and community—are what fill my tank, not empty calories.

Now I never panic about what's for dinner; my commitment is written daily to support me. It is always enough, and I know now that hunger is not an emergency. I love the simplicity because the sameness of my food keeps things automatic. I know I can do this, just for today, because I choose to. My right-sized body and sanity are so worth it!

Chapter 3

The Science
of a Simple Diet

Almost as soon as Bright Line Eating was launched there were people who were trying to make recipes that conformed to the Bright Lines *technically* but were basically stretching the Lines to their thinnest point. I'm looking at you, cauliflower pizza. And you, ricotta pancakes. The issue I have with these foods is that, while they are technically within the Lines, they are approaching food in a way that is antithetical to everything we are trying to accomplish. Spending time trying to solve a "food problem"—*How can I make pancakes and stay in my Bright Lines?*—is spending too much time on food. It's simply transferring your food chatter from obsessing about what you're going to eat to trying to get this new way of eating to hit all your old buttons. We are trying to get rid of the buttons!

Spending time with loved ones or spending time in service can hit your dopamine receptors in healthy ways. Exercise (once you're at goal weight) or physical intimacy will, too. But we are trying to take excess dopamine OUT of the food equation. If you are still trying to figure out how to get high off vegetables, you are not doing yourself any favors.

Our data shows that the people eating Bright Line food designed to mimic their old food don't get Happy, Thin, and Free. They report the slowest weight loss, the greatest frequency of cravings, and the most breaks in their Bright Lines of any group.

The reason we have curated the recipes in this book the way we have is that science strongly supports that eating simple foods helps our brains reset our Adiposity Set Point.

THE ADIPOSITY SET POINT

The Adiposity Set Point is the scientific name for what our brains think we should weigh. Its evolutionary function was to help us regain weight after illness or lose weight easily after childbirth. But now it serves as an invisible leg iron on the race to health. As an added challenge, it readjusts upward readily but fights tooth and nail against moving downward.

What we know now is that if the body releases significant weight but the Adiposity Set Point is never recalibrated to match, the brain will marshal a half dozen or more hormones—including our dear friend leptin, which it craters, and ghrelin, the hunger hormone, which it elevates—to create relentless hunger and cravings paired with a slowed metabolism . . . until the weight is regained.

In his 2017 book, *The Hungry Brain*,[1] neurobiology and obesity researcher Stephan J. Guyenet, Ph.D., writes about a 1965 experiment in which subjects were exclusively given a bland liquid (think viscous chalk water) to meet all their caloric needs. But they were entirely in charge of how much of it they could choose to drink each day. What researchers found was that the thin participants naturally consumed their typical calories and maintained their weight. However, the obese participants, some of whom voluntarily stayed on the regime as long as 255 days, could only push themselves to consume, at most, 400 calories a day. One person lost 200 pounds, or half his body weight. Most important, they reported *no hunger or cravings, ever.*

What was happening?

It turns out that a bland liquid diet allows people to shed excess fat without triggering the brain to fight back at all. It completely resets the Adiposity Set Point.

Now it's important to note this is not one of those commercial diets with a "shake for breakfast, shake for lunch" model. Those shakes are loaded with sugar or sugar substitutes and are in no way bland. What these subjects had was like drinking liquid cardboard.

How can we benefit from this without going on a liquid diet?

What scientists discovered after this study is that "satiety is sensory-specific." Meaning, we can feel full after the entrée but see the dessert and suddenly feel hungry again. The brain sees the new stimulus and kicks back into wanting. So continuing to switch up what we're offering ourselves keeps hunger, and accompanying cravings, alive.

Keeping food simple also resets the brain's expectation of what we should weigh.

My first encounter with this was through the Green Bean Women of Boston. In the 12-step food recovery world there are many programs with different structures and guidelines. I go into greater depth about this in my first book, but for this discussion I'm going to focus on the long-term recovery of those who have kept it simple. Overeaters Anonymous initially had a food plan called the Grey Sheet, named for the paper it was printed on. They distributed this diet to their members until 1986, when they stepped away from making specific food recommendations. But adherents to this diet are still out there today and I can usually pick them out in a meeting because, well into their 70s and 80s, they are still slender. And when conversation

turns to the exciting and exotic things to do with eggplant or the latest kitchen gizmo, one of them will quietly pipe up, "I just steam my green beans." Meaning, they have lasting peace around food by keeping their preparation simple and consistent. They are no longer looking for their food to "excite" them—because that leads down the road of keeping their addiction alive.

How simple is simple enough? Avoid the extremes. At one end, it would be to choose only three foods, eat only those, no salt, no spices, no seasoning of any kind. At the other extreme, it's mashing butternut squash and sweet potatoes together with pumpkin pie spice to try to evoke Thanksgiving. Find the middle ground. You know you've hit the sweet spot when—

→ You're getting free. The food chatter in your mind has quieted and your meals support your life, not the other way around.

→ It feels almost TOO easy. People who have struggled with their food for years often feel borderline freaked out to find their cravings disappear as their weight falls off.

→ You're not really all that hungry, just perhaps a bit before meals. That is a healthy biological cue.

→ Weight loss or goal-weight maintenance is happening.

Now, there are legitimate times when you're doing everything "right" and you still don't have the above. I strongly encourage you to lean into our support network if that happens. Join the online Boot Camp and get on a coaching call. But, in general, finding the sweet spot with simple food will produce calm, peace, and a feeling that healthy eating is getting EASIER.

"Simple food" can become an obsession too . . . don't feel guilty for using salt and pepper or some mustard sometimes. Really. But if you're needing 25 ingredients to make a meal, something's off.

In each chapter of this cookbook you will find that the recipes begin with the simplest ones people rely on in their weight-loss phase. Toward the end of each chapter, you will find more complex recipes with more ingredients. In addition to this progression from simple to more complex, each recipe has a trigger level rating—one bell, two bells, or three bells. One-bell recipes are safe, simple, and encouraged for newly initiated Bright Line Eaters. Once you have a few months of these new habits hardwired into your healing brain, you can experiment with some two-bell recipes. Once you're at goal weight, you may want to try the three-bell recipes. But know that if you ever try any recipe and find that sticking to your Lines in the hours or days after becomes harder, *that is not a recipe for you*. One person's neutral is another person's trigger. As you will see, we come back to this strongly around the subject of nut butter.

Most of us who were once obese and are now effortlessly maintaining slender bodies eat very simply. For example, most nights I eat a 14-ounce salad made up of the veggies I have in the house, plus either 4 ounces of tofu or 6 ounces of beans, plus ½ ounce of extra-virgin olive oil and some balsamic vinegar. It's super simple, and super consistent. But I love that salad. I enjoy it as much as, if not more than,

what I used to put in my mouth before Bright Line Eating because it has the added benefit of not only tasting delicious but being good for me on every level.

When I vlogged about the role of simple food in resetting the brain's Adiposity Set Point a year ago it set off an interesting furor in the Bright Line Eating community. Half of my viewers wrote to me in the weeks following to say, "Thank you. I just made my food simpler and I got FREE again!" About 40 percent of my responders said, "Amen. I keep my food simple already. It works." But then 10 percent said, "No, that messed me up. I tried to make my food simpler, as per your advice, and it threw me in the other direction. It became rapidly too restrictive and I found myself now wondering, *Is this simple enough?* It made me second-guess myself, when I had finally stopped doing that." Some people even broke their Bright Lines because they felt so destabilized or demoralized.

Obviously, then I would say, "Go back to whatever you were doing that was working. Do what gives you peace." This is the part where you need to be a scientist. Within your Bright Lines, if you are on weight loss, I encourage you to make your food simple enough to be NEUTRAL. That is always the ultimate goal for people who are high on the Susceptibility Scale: neutrality around food. We are trying to take the charge and the pull out of it completely. Science is showing that for a vast majority of people, eating simply supports that endeavor. But if you are in the 10 or so percent for whom that is not true, let it go.

The bottom line is this: Make your food simple enough to get free. You decide what that is. But trust us, it's simpler than the cauliflower pizza.

And finally, before we launch into the recipes themselves, I just want to mention one word: SURRENDER. Yup, surrender. Trust this plan. It's a whole new framework. A different kind of path. Instead of trying to keep your old relationship with food and force BLE into that framework, let go entirely and let us show you a new way. It may well feel scary, foreign, strange, and uncomfortable at first. But ultimately it's freeing, and I promise it will get easier.

DINA GROSSMAN

Before

After

STARTING DATE July 9, 2017
HEAVIEST WEIGHT 191 pounds
STARTING WEIGHT 187 pounds
GOAL WEIGHT ACHIEVED May 24, 2018
CURRENT WEIGHT 130 pounds
HEIGHT 5'2"

*B*efore BLE I cycled between bingeing and depriving myself. There were many healthy foods that I liked but could not work into my eating habits because I didn't have a clue about planning. So produce would rot in the fridge, and if I made beans, I didn't know how to manage large batches without eating them all at one time. When I hit bottom, I had stopped cooking and hated the thought of eating, which by that point brought very little genuine pleasure. In addition to periodically bingeing on addictive foods, at meals I gobbled very large quantities because it was my body screaming for real food after trying to starve myself. Finally, my wife had to do all the shopping and cooking—and we ate mindlessly in front of the TV.

The structure and massive support of Bright Line Eating have allowed me, at the age of 69, to become accomplished in basic adult self-care. I enjoy feeling competent. For the most part I enjoy my food and eat mindfully, meaning practically always at a table with cutlery. I even cut my fruit and eat it with a fork or spoon. If I find myself gobbling, I know I am on a slippery slope and strengthen my program with meditation, appreciation, and more careful planning.

After reaching my goal of 127 pounds, a series of binges pushed me a bit over. I am now learning to navigate maintenance more skillfully to better manage how and when I eat grains. Most important, the program has taught me that I have to avoid the exhaustion that can trigger crazy behavior. That is the difference in Bright Line Eating: I think. I am looking at not just *what* I eat now, but *when* and *how* I'm eating it. And I have a support community to hold me accountable.

Part Two

Bright Line
Recipes and
Techniques

Chapter 4

Bright Breakfasts

*B*efore we kick off Part II with breakfasts, I want to say a word about our Bright Lifers, who generously donated their recipes and wisdom. As you read their stories and look at their recipes, keep in mind that these Bright Lifers are real people who used to eat the way you've probably been eating.

As I talked to them about what they wanted to share with you, they remembered coming across Bright Line Eating for the first time and feeling hopeful, afraid, confused, and nervous, yet determined and willing to become people who have an entirely different relationship with food, just as you are now. Ours is one of the most generous and supportive communities on the planet. If you join us as a Bright Line eater, you may be afraid of what you're "giving up," but you'll be blown away by the deep connection and community waiting to welcome you.

Also, we'll say again that all the recipes presented here are portioned for women's weight loss. At the bottom of each recipe there are suggestions for adapting it for men's weight-loss portions.

You will also see some uses of the acronym NMF, which stands for Not My Food. We use that to describe what might be served at parties, or what we keep on hand to prepare for our children and spouses. It allows us to draw a hard, judgment-free boundary around it. It isn't good or bad, it just isn't ours.

The saying goes that breakfast is the most important meal of the day. In Bright Line Eating, kicking off the day by honoring the commitment we've made sets us up for confidence and success for the rest of the hours and meals to come.

Bright Line eaters love breakfasts as much as anyone. There's just something comforting about breakfast, right? Many of us settle into a breakfast we like and repeat it every day, choosing only to vary it, if at all, with the seasonal shifts in fresh fruit. It's automatic. It works. It gets our day off on the right foot.

When we polled our Bright Lifer volunteers for their favorite breakfast recipes, we discovered that there are a lot of oatmeal lovers among us. There are also quite a few who choose sweet potatoes instead of grains at breakfast.

So, since we had so many oatmeal and sweet potato recipes submitted, we've combined each of those into a main recipe, with many variations on that theme for you to choose from. In the rest, you'll see just one recipe at a time, credited to the Bright Lifer who lovingly submitted it.

Falafel with Yogurt Sauce

Recipe by *Shobha Tallapaka*

Number of Servings: **3** | Serving Size: **⅓ of Recipe** | Trigger Level: 🔔

EACH SERVING PROVIDES				
VEGETABLES	FRUIT	PROTEIN	FAT	GRAIN
6 OUNCES	**0 OUNCES**	**1 SERVING**	**0 SERVING**	**1 serving**

Falafel Ingredients

13½ ounces canned chickpeas, drained and crushed

12 ounces cooked quinoa

3 ounces onion, finely chopped

1½ ounces green chilies and fresh cilantro, finely chopped

Pinch each of salt and black pepper

1 teaspoon cumin

Yogurt Sauce Ingredients

6 ounces plain yogurt

13½ ounces grated cucumber (replacing breakfast fruit)

Pinch of salt

MEN'S OPTION No modifications.

Falafel Preparation

Preheat the oven to 375°F.

Line a baking sheet with parchment paper.

Combine the first four falafel ingredients into a bowl.

Add salt, pepper, and cumin.

Mash ingredients together.

Form the mixture into an even number of tight golf-ball-size balls. Place the falafel balls on the baking sheet and bake for 20 to 25 minutes.

Yogurt Sauce Preparation

Beat the yogurt with a fork until it is smooth and creamy.

Mix in the grated cucumber.

Season with salt.

Serve the falafel topped with the yogurt sauce.

Tip

We normally do not have vegetables for breakfast. In this recipe, the vegetables replace the fruit, which is an allowable modification but should never be done the other way around. You might also find it helpful to use a food processor to mash the chickpeas.

All About Oats

Compiled by *Molly Doogan*; recipes contributed by **Jana Allen, Nathan M. Denkin, Dee Holland-Vogt, Lisa Houser, Samantha Hughes, Anita Wicks Luther, Shanda McGrew, Sonja Schneider, Cindy Smith, Julie Boyd Smith, Mary Reisz,** and **Evelyn Zoecklein**

Number of Servings: **1** | Serving Size: **Entire Recipe** | Trigger Level: 🔔

EACH SERVING PROVIDES				
VEGETABLES	FRUIT	PROTEIN	FAT	GRAIN
0 ounces	6 ounces	1 serving	0 serving	1 serving

Ingredients

1 ounce total of one or more of the following: dry oats, grits, barley flakes, rye flakes, buckwheat flakes, quinoa flakes

4 ounces water

Select two items from the following list. Each item is ½ of a protein. You can choose two of the same item. If you are cooking your oats with milk, count that as one of your ½ proteins.

- 4 ounces unsweetened nonfat, low-fat, or full-fat milk, nut milk, or soy milk
- 1 ounce chopped, sliced, or whole nuts (almonds, pecans, walnuts, cashews, or pistachios) or 1 ounce nut butter
- 1 ounce seeds (chia, flax, hemp, pumpkin, or sunflower)
- 4 ounces plain yogurt (dairy, nondairy, sheep, goat, or Greek)

6 ounces fruit of your choice (berries, apples, or bananas work nicely)

MEN'S OPTION No modifications.

Preparation

Oats (steel-cut, old-fashioned rolled, or instant) can be batch cooked once a week or cooked fresh daily. The basic ratio for cooking is 1:4 of dry oats to liquid. If you batch cook, weigh out 4 ounces to equal 1 grain serving.

Cook 1 ounce of oats (equals 1 grain) with 4 ounces of water according to the directions on the package for the stove top, microwave, or pressure cooker.

Top with your two selected ½ protein and 6 ounces fruit.

 Tip Look for interesting grain flake variations in the bulk section of your local health food store.

Variations

- **Creamy Oatmeal:** For a creamier oatmeal base, cook the grain in 4 ounces milk instead of water. This will modify your protein allowance in the recipe by ½.
- **Apple Spice Oatmeal:** Mix oats, milk, nuts, spices, and salt. Cook over medium heat for 9 to 15 minutes, stirring occasionally, until thick. Top with chopped apples.
- **Banana Berry:** Microwave your fruit for 2 minutes. Mix in a serving of precooked oats and microwave an additional 1 minute. Top with yogurt and nuts.
- **Banana–Nut Butter Oats:** Cook 1 ounce of oats with 4 ounces of milk or water. Remove from the heat and stir in 1 ounce of nut butter and spices. Add 6 ounces of chopped or mashed banana.
- **Overnight Oats:** Add 1 ounce of oats to a bowl (rolled or instant oats work best). Mix in 2 ounces of milk. Layer in 6 ounces of fresh or frozen fruit and top with 4 ounces of yogurt. Cover and refrigerate. In the morning, add ½ ounce of nuts or seeds before eating cold.

Bright Breakfasts

Sweet Potato Breakfast

Compiled by *Charlotte Coit*, recipes contributed by **Susan Cook, Beth Syverson, and Erin Wallace**

Number of Servings: **1** | Serving Size: **Entire Recipe** | Trigger Level:

EACH SERVING PROVIDES

VEGETABLES	FRUIT	PROTEIN	FAT	GRAIN
0 ounces	6 ounces	1 serving	0 serving	1 serving

Ingredients

4 ounces baked sweet potato

1 ounce nut butter

½ ounce chopped nuts

⅕ ounce ground flaxseeds

³⁄₁₀ ounce hemp seeds

¼ teaspoon cinnamon

6 ounces mixed berries

Preparation

Preheat the oven to 375°F. Line a baking sheet with parchment paper.

Wash and scrub the sweet potato clean, then cut it in half lengthwise. Place the sweet potato, cut side down, on the baking sheet. Bake until you see caramelized edges on the cut sides.

Weigh 4 ounces of the cooked sweet potato.

While the sweet potato is still hot, split each side open and add the nut butter so it melts a little. Top with chopped nuts, seeds, cinnamon, and berries. Can be vegan or vegetarian.

MEN'S OPTION No modifications.

 A baked sweet potato will keep in the fridge for at least 3 days.

Variations

- Instead of berries, use 6 ounces of chopped or mashed banana or peach.
- Instead of flax and hemp seeds, use ½ ounce of chopped pecans or slivered almonds.
- Instead of cinnamon, try pumpkin spice, ginger, nutmeg, or vanilla powder.
- Instead of 1 ounce nut butter, use 4 ounces of plain Greek yogurt.

Cottage Cheese, Cereal, and Berries

Recipe by *Amanda Michelle Albright*

*"Every week, I fill up a Tupperware with washed and chopped berries,
so it's a breeze to put this together in the morning."*

Number of Servings: **1** | Serving Size: **Entire Recipe** | Trigger Level: 🔔🔔

EACH SERVING PROVIDES

VEGETABLES	FRUIT	PROTEIN	FAT	GRAIN
0 ounces	6 ounces	1 serving	0 serving	1 serving

Ingredients

4 ounces cottage cheese

6 ounces berries (blueberries, blackberries, and/or chopped strawberries)

1 ounce no-sugar, high-fiber cereal flakes

Preparation

Mix all the ingredients in a bowl and serve.

MEN'S OPTION Use 6 ounces of cottage cheese per serving.

Rice Cakes and Nut Butter

Recipe by *Lisa Houser*

"This recipe is great when you're on the go!"

Number of Servings: **1** | Serving Size: **Entire Recipe** | Trigger Level: 🔔🔔🔔

EACH SERVING PROVIDES

VEGETABLES	FRUIT	PROTEIN	FAT	GRAIN
0 ounces	1 serving	1 serving	0 serving	1 serving

Ingredients

2 ounces nut butter

1 ounce rice cakes

1 banana or apple, sliced

Preparation

Spread the nut butter on your rice cakes.

Top with banana or apple slices.

MEN'S OPTION No modifications.

Variations

➤ **Women:** Substitute 2 hard-boiled eggs for the nut butter and serve with 6 ounces of berries on the side instead of banana or apple.

➤ **Men:** Substitute 3 hard-boiled eggs for the nut butter and serve with 6 ounces of berries on the side instead of banana or apple.

Note

This recipe is only recommended for people for whom nut butter is a neutral food. If you find after eating this that you have increased food chatter or increased cravings, either try it with a nut butter you can tolerate, or don't use this recipe.

Breakfast Parfait

Recipe by *Marian Walters*

Number of Servings: **1** | Serving Size: **Entire Recipe** | Trigger Level: 🔔

EACH SERVING PROVIDES

VEGETABLES	FRUIT	PROTEIN	FAT	GRAIN
0 ounces	6 ounces	¾ serving	0 serving	1 serving

Ingredients

1 ounce dry oatmeal

6 ounces plain yogurt

6 ounces blueberries

Preparation

Mix 1 ounce oatmeal with 2 to 3 ounces water; microwave for 1 to 2 minutes. Add more water for a thinner consistency.

Place ⅓ of the cooked oatmeal in a bowl or parfait glass. Layer ⅓ of the yogurt on top of the oatmeal. Top with ⅓ of the blueberries. Repeat two times.

MEN'S OPTION No modifications.

Tip

For a full serving of protein, use 2 ounces of milk in your coffee, add ½ ounce nuts or seeds, or increase the yogurt to 8 ounces.

Breakfast Quinoa

Recipe by *Lisa Houser*

Number of Servings: **1** | Serving Size: **Entire Recipe** | Trigger Level: 🔔

EACH SERVING PROVIDES

VEGETABLES	FRUIT	PROTEIN	FAT	GRAIN
0 ounces	1 serving	1 serving	0 serving	1 serving

Ingredients

1 banana

4 ounces cooked quinoa

4 ounces almond milk or other nondairy milk

1 ounce hemp hearts

MEN'S OPTION   No modifications.

Preparation

Mash the banana together with the cooked quinoa in a bowl.

Allow the mixture to set overnight.

In the morning, add the milk and hemp hearts.

Microwave for 1½ to 2 minutes on high.

Chia Pudding

Recipe by *Erin Wallace*

Number of Servings: **1** | Serving Size: **Entire Recipe** | Trigger Level: 🔔

EACH SERVING PROVIDES

VEGETABLES	FRUIT	PROTEIN	FAT	GRAIN
0 ounces	6 ounces	1 serving	0 serving	1 serving

Ingredients

1 ounce dry oats

½ ounce chia seeds

6 ounces milk

¼ teaspoon vanilla extract (optional)

Pinch of cinnamon

6 ounces fruit of choice

MEN'S OPTION   No modifications.

Preparation

Combine all the ingredients except the fruit in a mason jar and shake well.

Leave in the refrigerator overnight to thicken.

In the morning, transfer the pudding to a bowl and top with the fruit of your choice.

Tip   For a warm breakfast, heat the pudding in the microwave.

Grab-and-Go PB&J

Recipe by *Julie Boyd Smith*

Number of Servings: **1** | Serving Size: **Entire Recipe** | Trigger Level: 🔔🔔🔔

EACH SERVING PROVIDES

VEGETABLES	FRUIT	PROTEIN	FAT	GRAIN
0 ounces	6 ounces	1 serving	0 serving	1 serving

Ingredients

3 ounces frozen banana, thawed

2 ounces peanut butter

1 ounce dry oatmeal

3 ounces frozen cherries

Preparation

Move the banana to one side of the bowl in which it was thawed. Mix the peanut butter with the liquid from the thawed banana.

Mash and mix the banana into the peanut butter. Add the oatmeal and then the frozen cherries.

Transfer the mixture to a sandwich-size plastic bag and roll into a large log. Store in the freezer.

To eat, simply remove from the freezer, peel back the plastic, and enjoy! Or you can wait for it to thaw and then eat.

MEN'S OPTION No modifications.

Tip This recipe is only recommended for people for whom peanut butter is a neutral food. If you find after eating this that you have increased food chatter or increased cravings, either try it with a nut butter you can tolerate, or don't use this recipe.

Beans, Sweet Potatoes, and Apples, Oh My!

Recipe by *Debby Edwards*

"This recipe travels well and is very filling.
I have put this in a wide-mouth thermos
and taken it on the plane with me!"

Number of Servings: **1** | Serving Size: **Entire Recipe** | Trigger Level:

EACH SERVING PROVIDES

VEGETABLES	FRUIT	PROTEIN	FAT	GRAIN
0 ounces	**6 ounces**	**1 serving**	**0 serving**	**1 serving**

Ingredients

6 ounces cooked black beans (or your choice of beans)

6 ounces Granny Smith apple, chopped

4 ounces cooked purple sweet potato (steamed or oven baked without oil)

Pinch each of ground cardamom, cinnamon, ginger, and nutmeg

Preparation

Heat your beans on the stove top, in the microwave, or in a pressure cooker, and keep them warm while you are chopping up your apple.

Heat your sweet potato.

Place the apple pieces on your plate. Scoop the sweet potatoes on top of the apples and then top with the beans and spices.

MEN'S OPTION No modifications.

Variation

➤ Use 1 ounce of grits or polenta instead of the sweet potatoes.

Ricotta Oats in a Jar

Recipe by *Evelyn Zoecklein*

Number of Servings: **1** | Serving Size: **Entire Recipe** | Trigger Level: 🔔🔔

EACH SERVING PROVIDES				
VEGETABLES	FRUIT	PROTEIN	FAT	GRAIN
0 ounces	**6 ounces**	**1 serving**	**0 serving**	**1 serving**

Ingredients

1 ounce old-fashioned oats (not quick oats)

2 ounces ricotta cheese

6 ounces frozen blueberries (or your favorite fruit)

1 teaspoon cinnamon

1 teaspoon pumpkin spice

1 ounce sliced almonds

Preparation

Place the oats, ricotta cheese, and blueberries in a widemouthed pint-size mason jar.

Add water to cover the blueberries.

Microwave for 3 minutes.

Sprinkle in the spices and stir.

Microwave for an additional 1 minute.

Stir in the almonds.

Let sit for 5 minutes before serving.

MEN'S OPTION   Use 3 ounces of ricotta cheese per serving.

Cheese and Rice Omelet

Recipe by *Julie Boyd Smith*

Number of Servings: **1** | Serving Size: **Entire Recipe** | Trigger Level:

EACH SERVING PROVIDES

VEGETABLES	FRUIT	PROTEIN	FAT	GRAIN
0 ounces	0 ounces	1 serving	0 serving	1 serving

Ingredients

1 ounce shredded cheddar cheese

1 egg

4 ounces cooked rice

Preparation

Whisk the shredded cheese and egg together in a small bowl.

Warm the rice in a small nonstick pan over medium-high heat.

When the rice is heated through, create a hole in the center and pour in the egg mixture.

Immediately start scrambling the egg mixture into the rice mixture and keep turning every 10 seconds or so until the egg is cooked and the shredded cheese is melted.

MEN'S OPTION Use 2 eggs per serving.

Variation

→ If you want the dish to be more like fried rice than an omelet, allow the egg mixture to cook a bit longer before you mix it with the rice.

Sunday Breakfast Rustic Patties

Recipe by *Josie Colicchia*

Number of Servings: **1** | Serving Size: **Entire Recipe** | Trigger Level: 🔔

EACH SERVING PROVIDES

VEGETABLES	FRUIT	PROTEIN	FAT	GRAIN
0 ounces	6 ounces	1 serving	0 serving	1 serving

Ingredients

4 ounces steamed sweet potato

2 ounces banana

1 egg

1½ ounces cooked lentils

1 teaspoon cinnamon (optional)

2 ounces yogurt

**4 ounces blueberries
(fresh or frozen)**

Preparation

Lightly mash the sweet potato and banana together with a fork. Crack the egg and mix it in well.

Add the lentils and combine the mixture, adding the cinnamon if you like.

Preheat a large nonstick pan over medium heat. Add the mixture to the pan in large spoonfuls (you can make the patties as large or small as you like).

Cook the patties on medium heat for 2 to 3 minutes per side.

Serve the patties topped with yogurt and blueberries.

MEN'S OPTION Use 2 eggs per serving.

Spanish Eggs

Recipe by *Maria Ines Segret*

Number of Servings: **1** | Serving Size: **Entire Recipe** | Trigger Level: 🔔🔔

EACH SERVING PROVIDES

VEGETABLES	FRUIT	PROTEIN	FAT	GRAIN
0 ounces	6 ounces	1 serving	0 serving	1 serving

Ingredients

Enough potatoes to yield 4 ounces cooked (approximately 1 medium potato)

2 eggs

Pinch of salt

Oil spray

Pinch of chili powder (optional)

6 ounces of mixed berries

Preparation

Peel the potatoes (optional) and cut them into thin slices. Boil the potato slices until they are cooked through, approximately 7 minutes.

Crack the eggs into a mixing bowl. Season with salt and whisk together.

When the potatoes are cooked, weigh 4 ounces and add them into the eggs.

Spray a little bit of oil in a small pan and place it over medium heat. When the pan is hot, add the egg and potato mixture.

Cook until the bottom part of the mixture is done, approximately 1 to 2 minutes; then flip it over and cook the other side for 1 minute more. Top with chili powder, if using.

Serve with berries as shown for a complete breakfast meal.

MEN'S OPTION Use 3 eggs per serving.

Sweet Potato Fruit Bake

Recipe by *Sharon Mack*

Number of Servings: **4** | Serving Size: **¼ of Recipe** | Trigger Level: 🔔🔔🔔

EACH SERVING PROVIDES

VEGETABLES	FRUIT	PROTEIN	FAT	GRAIN
0 ounces	6 ounces	1 serving	0 serving	1 serving

Ingredients

16 ounces cooked sweet potato without skin

4 ounces banana

2 eggs

¼ teaspoon sea salt

4 ounces almond milk

1 ounce flaxseed

8 ounces chopped apple

1 teaspoon cinnamon

⅛ teaspoon ground cloves

4 ounces pecans or walnuts

12 ounces fruit of your choice

Preparation

Preheat the oven to 350°F.

Mash the sweet potatoes in a large bowl with a fork. Add the banana and mash together.

Whisk the eggs and ¼ teaspoon salt in a separate bowl. Add the almond milk and mix together.

Add the egg mixture to the sweet potato mixture. Add the flaxseed, apple, cinnamon, and ground cloves, mixing until well combined.

Pour the mixture into an 8x8-inch baking dish. Top with the nuts, covering equally.

Bake for 30 minutes. Allow to cool thoroughly before cutting.

Top with fruit and serve cold.

MEN'S OPTION Use 3 eggs per serving.

Banana Rice Bake

Recipe by *Nikki VanDenHeuvel*

Number of Servings: **1** | Serving Size: **Entire Recipe** | Trigger Level: 🔔🔔

EACH SERVING PROVIDES

VEGETABLES	FRUIT	PROTEIN	FAT	GRAIN
0 ounces	6 ounces	1 serving	0 serving	1 serving

Ingredients

6 ounces banana, mashed

1 egg

4 ounces cooked rice

4 ounces milk of your choice

½ teaspoon vanilla extract (optional)

½ teaspoon cinnamon

Oil spray

Preparation

Preheat the oven to 350°F.

Place all the ingredients in a bowl and mix to combine.

Spray an 8x8-inch baking dish with oil. Pour the mixture into the dish.

Bake for 20 minutes.

MEN'S OPTION Use 2 eggs per serving

Oatmeal Rounds

Recipe by *Valerie Proctor-Conner*

Number of Servings: **1** | Serving Size: **Entire Recipe** | Trigger Level: 🔔🔔🔔

EACH SERVING PROVIDES

VEGETABLES	FRUIT	PROTEIN	FAT	GRAIN
0 ounces	6 ounces	1 serving	0 serving	1 serving

Ingredients

4 ounces cooked steel-cut oats

1 egg

1 ounce chopped pecans

1 teaspoon vanilla extract (optional)

Pinch of cinnamon

Pinch of nutmeg

Pinch of cardamom

Oil spray

6 ounces cherries

Preparation

Mix all the ingredients, except the cherries, together in a bowl to make a thick batter.

Lightly spray griddle with oil.

Drop ¼ cup of the batter onto the hot griddle. (The batter should yield three rounds.)

Cook 2 minutes on each side.

Top with cherries.

MEN'S OPTION Use 2 eggs per serving.

JENNIFER DOONAN

Before

After

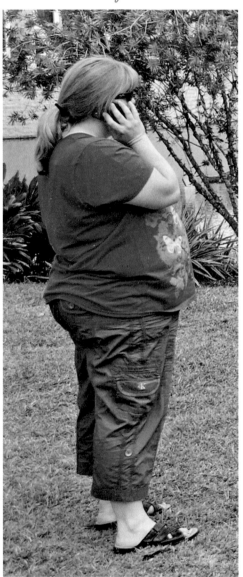

STARTING DATE **October 11, 2016**
HEAVIEST WEIGHT **240 pounds**
STARTING WEIGHT **204 pounds**
GOAL WEIGHT ACHIEVED **July 16, 2017**
CURRENT WEIGHT **133 pounds**
HEIGHT **5'3"**

I have struggled with weight my whole life. By the time I married I was 190 pounds, and once we started having kids, I gained more and more weight. I wasn't eating healthy. No veggies at all and little to no fruit. Mostly fast food and processed food. Even on diets, I would save all my points during the day to eat treats and highly processed foods at night. I was prediabetic, had liver issues, blood pressure issues, bone spurs in my heels, bursitis in my hip, and had constant knee pain.

Then my dad got colon cancer. It was like a lightning bolt hit me and I realized I was killing myself. I started eating salads and healthy, organic foods and lost 74 pounds. I was very excited. I thought, *This is the answer I was waiting for.* But soon I started experimenting with organic desserts and vegan treats. Basically I just made my addiction organic, and eventually I stopped losing weight.

I increased my exercise to see if that would help me, but then I blew out my knee. My dreams of getting to my goal weight were dwindling. I started to realize for the first time that I have a food addiction. I had thought if I could just eat healthy, then I would be healthy. But I was still not able to control my food. I was back over 200 again. And I knew I would be back at 240 soon.

Fast-forward to now, one year on maintenance, and I feel wonderful. I am truly free. Is it easy all the time? No. But is it easy most of the time? YES!! There are still those moments that I struggle, but I WORK the program. I reach out, I seek help, I don't put the food in my mouth. Eating is not the fix. Sticking to my Lines is the fix. Now I can order clothes online and they fit every time. I can sit comfortably, walk, ride a bike, and live an active, adventurous lifestyle. I have so much energy from the time I wake up until I go to bed. My A1C is 4.6. My liver is healthy. My body is healthy. My mind is at peace.

I can feel the hope, fear, tears, and anticipation that you are feeling right now. I remember feeling this exact same way. I remember reading other posts like this one, thinking, *Is this really possible for me?* Let me encourage you that it is most definitely possible—100 percent possible. Believe, seek, trust, and go for it. You'll never regret it.

Chapter 5

All about Vegetables

Before we can go any further with the rest of your Bright Line day we have to stop and talk about vegetables. Vegetables are the bedrock of Bright Line Eating. But what I have found over the years is that many people come into Bright Line Eating with no idea how to prepare them. Either they've been living on meal-replacement bars or eating so much flour and sugar that vegetables have gradually exited their diet completely, or their idea of salads is wilted iceberg lettuce with creamy high-calorie, high-fat dressing and bacon bits.

We are here to reintroduce you to the tasty, satisfying, nutritious, filling world of vegetables. Our preparations are very basic, yes. But they are easy and delicious. Below you will find many ways to batch prep vegetables that you can keep on hand to add to your warm bowls and cold bowls to make them sing. So these are not recipes for whole meals but rather ways to prepare the vegetable part of your meals that will wow your palate, fill your belly, and heal your body and brain.

We will kick things off with quotes from our Bright Lifers about their journey with vegetables. Maybe some of what they say will resonate with you.

Also note, in this chapter we won't be making conversions for men's portions because you will just add as many ounces of vegetables as your personal plan allows.

Enjoy!

- -

"Prior to BLE I rarely ate vegetables. Now I think of vegetables
as my power food. My body thrives on them."

— *Jodi Maile*

- -

- -

"Pre-BLE I would make one smallish bowl of veggies for my family and
me to share. Now I wear a big ol' BLE badge of honor when I get to eat
a ton of veggies at each meal; the more variety the better."

— *Jodie McDowell*

- -

"I was such a carboholic, I never thought I'd get used to
the overwhelming, nauseating piles of vegetables.
Now? I am absolutely gleeful looking at my
overflowing plate of colors, textures, and tastes!"

— *Ellen Eichen Weinman*

"I remember the first few BLE dinners, my wife and I would look at each
other toward the end of the meal and say, 'Just keep chewing!'
Still, even a year and a half later, there are some nights
that 14 ounces of vegetables evokes from one of us,
'Just keep chewing!'"

— *Kent Rappleye*

"I hated veggies before BLE and hardly ate any.
Now I love them and crave them and get very upset
if I don't get my quota for the day!"

— *Leslee Carr Feiwus*

"My early days found me naively making a 14-ounce leafy salad and laughing hysterically at the ridiculous pile it made. I admit I'm still eating just 8 ounces of dinner vegetables and loving far more varieties of vegetables than I ever imagined."

— *Susan Cook*

"I was shocked. I thought, *You've got to be kidding,* and could only force down 10 ounces at dinner. Now I have explored all kinds of veggies and preparation methods and love them—and can handle the full 14 ounces."

— *Sue Mack Gaulke*

"Six ounces of vegetables at lunch was easy, but that 14 ounces at dinner was only a suggestion . . . right?! Now, over a year in, I easily eat 14 ounces at both lunch and dinner!"

— *Molly Doogan*

"I like soup in the winter, and it's easy
to make if I have some vegetable stock ready.
During the summer months, I take the 'waste' parts of my veggies
(the hearts of the cauliflower, stems of chard, ends of carrots, etc.)
and put them in freezer bags. When I'm ready for soup,
I take those out of the freezer and add water to a pot.
I'll often add some yellow onion as well. I let the broth simmer for
about an hour. Then I use a strainer to strain the vegetable parts out.
And voilà: ready-made vegetable stock!"

— *Julia Carol*

"I really love spaghetti squash, but wanted to minimize
the prep time and move on from my old way of preparing it—
with lots of butter or oil. To cook spaghetti squash in the microwave,
poke several holes with a fork like you would do to a potato.
Cook the squash in the microwave for 10 to 12 minutes, depending
on the size. Let it sit for a couple of minutes until it's
cool enough to handle. Cut the squash in half lengthwise,
remove and discard the seeds, and then scoop out
the flesh to be weighed and eaten!"

— *Michelle Pecharich*

"Before BLE my husband would say,
'We need to eat more veggies,' and I'd reply, 'Yuck.'
Now he says, 'I can't eat any more veggies,' and I reply,
'What? I LOVE them and wish I could have more!'"

— Ellen Moyer

"My biggest problem when I started BLE was,
'How in the world am I ever going to eat 20 ounces of vegetables a
day?' I experimented with all sorts of new veggies and preparation
methods—from grilling to sautéing, steaming to roasting, etc.
Now I *love* vegetables!"

—Sue Mack Gaulke

"Before BLE, I hated cutting veggies for a salad.
It has now become part of my dinner routine
and almost feels meditative!"

— Mary Judkins

"When I began BLE, I tried to eat 14 ounces of romaine lettuce for
dinner. This required a mixing bowl and 45 minutes of chewing!
I was exhausted, until I gave it more thought and saw great tips
from others on the Boot Camp Facebook page.
Now I adore my vegetables at dinner, which generally
consists of 4 ounces romaine or leafy green lettuce,
2 ounces bell pepper strips, and 2 ounces grape tomatoes,
along with 6 ounces delicious cooked vegetable of the day."

— *Peggy Mowry*

"To make kale less tough and also less bitter,
massage the kale with a splash of lemon juice.
The splash of lemon juice also makes
red cabbage and arugula less strongly flavored."

— *Julia Carol*

STORING YOUR FRESH VEGETABLES

This is one of those things that flummoxes so many people in the beginning, so we are going to break it down for you.

Greens (lettuces, spinach, collard greens, turnip or beet greens, arugula): Wash them gently in very cold water, then wrap up in a slightly moist towel and refrigerate. Or buy them prewashed in bags and they're ready to use!

Tomatoes: Keep out of the refrigerator for better texture and flavor. Tomatoes are a fruit and will keep ripening after they've been picked. Note that tomatoes are counted as vegetables in the Bright Line Eating food plan.

Carrots/Celery/Radishes: All of these will last longer and resist getting rubbery if you cut away the greens, cover the root vegetables in water, and refrigerate in a covered container. Carrots can be frozen if parboiled first; then you can add them to soup.

Green Beans/Edamame/Sugar Snap or Snow Peas: Gently wash in cold water and store in a plastic, nylon, or linen bag in the refrigerator. Note that edamame is counted as a protein in the Bright Line Eating food plan.

Basil/Cilantro/Parsley/Dill: Cut off about ½ inch of the bottom of the stems (so they'll continue to take in water through the stem) and add to a glass of water on the counter. Do not refrigerate. Change the water daily. You can use scissors to snip off the amount of the herbs you want to use.

Summer Squashes (zucchini, pattypan, straightneck, crookneck, etc.): These may be stored in the refrigerator or left on the counter if they'll be cooked soon. If refrigerated, leave them unwashed until you're ready to cook them.

Winter Squashes (butternut, acorn, pumpkin, spaghetti, etc.): Leave outside of the refrigerator; these will last quite a while before you have to cook them.

Broccoli/Cauliflower/Brussels Sprouts/Parsnips/Turnips: These should be cooked soon after purchasing. They may be stored whole with a moist towel wrapped around them. Parsnips and turnips also store well in a cool, dry place, like a root cellar.

FREEZING

Spring and summer often have the best variety of vegetables. Consider shopping at a farmers' market or fresh produce store and freezing some of your favorites for winter or fall. Freezing is also great for leftovers, in the event you end up with too many vegetables to eat before they go bad.

In general, any vegetable you can buy frozen in the supermarket is a vegetable you can freeze yourself from leftovers at home. Except for corn, which may be frozen raw, vegetables need to be cooked, or at least parboiled, before freezing. To parboil, simply boil the vegetable for a few minutes and then allow it to cool off before freezing it in a relatively airtight container. If you have a countertop vacuum sealer, those are great, too.

It's great to have frozen veggies on hand so that you're ready for that busy week when you didn't have time to shop and need some veggies for your next day's Bright Line meal plan!

To freeze fresh lemons, cut them into quarters or slices, lay them out on a flat baking sheet, and set them in the freezer. Once frozen, you can put them in freezer bags for storage. They'll last a few months.

While it's true that you can freeze avocados, they do lose some of their texture, so thawed avocado is best for guacamole or in a dressing. To freeze, mash up the avocado and add a little lemon, then put it into a freezer-safe container. It will last a few months.

GENERAL PREP

Always wash and dry your fresh produce, unless it comes in packaging that specifies otherwise, like triple-washed arugula.

Spiralized veggies make a great pasta replacement, and you will see recipes here with sauce and cheese. Some of the vegetables that make good "noodles" are parsnips, turnips, carrots, zucchini, yellow squash, sweet potatoes, and peeled broccoli stems.

To replace tortillas and bread, collard or other large green leaves make great wraps. Combine a meat or bean mixture with chopped veggies and sauce and use a big leaf of Napa cabbage or collard green to roll it into a wrap.

Roasting is one of the most delicious ways to eat vegetables. Many Bright Lifers found their way into loving vegetables by beginning with roasted veggies. Caution: For those who are super-high on the Susceptibility Scale, roasted vegetables can taste soooo good that they're a trigger to break the Quantities Line! So . . . once again, know yourself and take responsibility for meal planning in the best way for your program.

Basic Roasted Vegetables for All Seasons

Recipe by *Julie Boyd Smith*

Number of Servings: **Multiple** | Serving Size: **6 ounces** | Trigger Level: 🔔

EACH SERVING PROVIDES

VEGETABLES	FRUIT	PROTEIN	FAT	GRAIN
6 ounces	0 ounces	0 serving	0 serving	0 serving

Spring/Summer Ingredients

1 onion

3 red peppers

1 fennel bulb

1 summer squash

1 tablespoon balsamic vinegar

Pinch each of salt and black pepper

Spring/Summer Preparation

Preheat the oven to 425°F.

Cut the vegetables into ¾-inch slices and place them in a single layer on a rimmed baking sheet.

Drizzle the balsamic vinegar and sprinkle the salt and pepper over the vegetables.

Roast for 25 to 35 minutes until lightly browned.

Weigh 6 ounces of cooked vegetables for a women's weight-loss lunch portion.

Fall/Winter Ingredients

1 bunch carrots

1 bunch parsnips

½ pound brussels sprouts

1 eggplant

1 tablespoon balsamic vinegar

Pinch each of salt and black pepper

Fall/Winter Preparation

Preheat the oven to 425°F.

Cut the vegetables into large, 1-inch-thick slices and place them in a single layer on a rimmed baking sheet.

Drizzle the balsamic vinegar and sprinkle the salt and pepper over the vegetables.

Roast for 30 to 40 minutes until lightly browned.

MEN'S OPTION No modifications.

All about Vegetables

Roasted Cauliflower

Recipe by *Julia Carol*

Number of Servings: **Multiple** | Serving Size: **6 ounces** | Trigger Level: 🔔

EACH SERVING PROVIDES				
VEGETABLES	FRUIT	PROTEIN	FAT	GRAIN
6 ounces	**0 ounces**	**0 serving**	**0 serving**	**0 serving**

Ingredients

1 head of cauliflower

Olive oil spray

1 lemon

1 to 2 tablespoons nutritional yeast

Salt and black pepper

Preparation

Preheat the oven to 350°F. Line a baking sheet with parchment paper.

Cut the cauliflower into 2-inch chunks and place in a bowl. Mist the cauliflower with olive oil spray and toss to coat.

Spread the cauliflower out on the baking sheet and roast for about 40 minutes, or until the cauliflower is beginning to brown.

Remove the cauliflower from the oven and squeeze lemon juice over the top, followed by a sprinkling of nutritional yeast.

Season with salt and pepper to taste.

Weigh 6 ounces of cooked vegetables for a women's weight-loss lunch portion.

MEN'S OPTION No modifications.

Variation

➜ This method of roasting may be done with broccoli. Don't use the lemon juice, but everything else can stay the same. The nutritional yeast sprinkled on top is delicious!

Charred Green Beans

Recipe by *Louise Giffels*

Number of Servings: **1** | Serving Size: **Entire Recipe** | Trigger Level: 🔔

EACH SERVING PROVIDES

VEGETABLES	FRUIT	PROTEIN	FAT	GRAIN
6 ounces	0 ounces	0 serving	1 serving	0 serving

Ingredients

6 ounces green beans

½ ounce oil

Salt and black pepper

Preparation

Toss the green beans with the oil in a bowl.

Heat a large cast-iron skillet until very hot.

Place the beans in the skillet, cover, and cook for 4 minutes.

Stir the beans and continue cooking for another 3 to 4 minutes until they are charred and tender.

Season with salt and pepper.

MEN'S OPTION No modifications.

Cinnamon Winter Squash

Recipe by *Evelyn Ziegler*

Number of Servings: **Multiple** | Serving Size: **6 ounces** | Trigger Level: 🔔

EACH SERVING PROVIDES

VEGETABLES	FRUIT	PROTEIN	FAT	GRAIN
6 ounces	**0 ounces**	**0 serving**	**0 serving**	**0 serving**

Ingredients

Olive oil spray

1 bag precut winter squash (butternut, acorn, etc.)

Pinch of salt

Pinch of cinnamon

Preparation

Preheat the oven to 400°F.

Coat a baking sheet lightly with olive oil spray.

Spread out the squash on the baking sheet.

Sprinkle with salt and cinnamon.

Bake until the squash is soft, about 30 minutes. Halfway through, flip the pieces over and shuffle them around.

Weigh 6 ounces of cooked vegetables for a women's weight-loss lunch portion.

MEN'S OPTION No modifications.

Tip Keep the baked squash in the fridge and measure what you need for your vegetable portions.

Roasted Asparagus with Kumquats and Almonds

Recipe by *Julia Carol*

Number of Servings: **1** | Serving Size: **Entire Recipe** | Trigger Level: 🔔🔔

EACH SERVING PROVIDES

VEGETABLES	FRUIT	PROTEIN	FAT	GRAIN
6 ounces	6 ounces	½ serving	0 serving	0 serving

Ingredients

**Enough asparagus to yield
6 ounces cooked**

3 large garlic cloves, diced

Olive oil spray

1 ounce slivered almonds

6 ounces kumquats

**1 teaspoon balsamic vinegar
(optional)**

Salt and black pepper

Preparation

Preheat the oven to 400°F. Line a baking sheet with parchment paper.

Wash the asparagus and snap off the ends. Place the asparagus in a single layer on the baking sheet.

Sprinkle the garlic on top of the asparagus. Mist the vegetables with olive oil spray.

Roast for about 15 minutes, depending on the thickness of the asparagus.

While the asparagus is roasting, lightly toast the almonds in a toaster oven or in a small frying pan.

Cut the kumquats in half.

Remove the asparagus from the oven, weigh out 6 ounces and place on plate.

Sprinkle the toasted almonds on top and drizzle with balsamic vinegar, if desired.

Top or surround the dish with the kumquats, season with salt and pepper, and serve.

MEN'S OPTION No modifications.

Slow-Cooker Southern-Style Green Beans

Recipe by *Heidi Stallman*

*"I can throw this together
in less than five minutes in the morning."*

Number of Servings: **Multiple** | Serving Size: **6 ounces** | Trigger Level: 🔔

EACH SERVING PROVIDES

VEGETABLES	FRUIT	PROTEIN	FAT	GRAIN
6 ounces	**0 ounces**	**0 serving**	**0 serving**	**0 serving**

Ingredients

**2 pounds fresh or frozen snapped
and cut green beans**

1 large onion, diced

1 cup water

1 tablespoon minced garlic

1 teaspoon ground black pepper

Pinch of salt

¼ teaspoon cayenne pepper (optional)

Preparation

Place all the ingredients in a slow cooker, mix well, and cook on high for 4 hours or low for up to 10 hours.

Weigh 6 ounces of cooked vegetables for a women's weight-loss lunch portion.

MEN'S OPTION No modifications.

Variations

➛ Add a splash of hot sauce if you like!

➛ Add ½ ounce olive oil to your weighed portion after cooking to add 1 fat serving.

➛ This recipe also works great with turnip, collard, or mustard greens.

➛ You may also enjoy adding a single slice of ham to the pot. I remove the ham at the end, weigh out 4 ounces, and eat it as my lunch protein with the green beans or leafy greens on the side.

Pickled Beets

Recipe by *Ellen Eichen Weinman*

Number of Servings: **Multiple** | Serving Size: **6 ounces** | Trigger Level: 🔔

EACH SERVING PROVIDES

VEGETABLES	FRUIT	PROTEIN	FAT	GRAIN
6 ounces	0 ounces	0 serving	0 serving	0 serving

Ingredients

1 pound beets

½ cup apple cider vinegar

½ teaspoon mustard powder

Preparation

Remove the greens, trim the roots, and wash the beets thoroughly.

Steam the beets on the stove top for 22 to 25 minutes until tender.

Rinse the cooked beets under cold water and peel off the skin.

Mix the vinegar and mustard powder in a large bowl.

Slice or quarter the beets into bite-size pieces and add to the vinegar mixture. Let the beets cool, stirring every 30 minutes or so.

Refrigerate once cool. Wait at least 2 days before enjoying, stirring a couple of times to make sure all the pieces get coated.

Weigh 6 ounces for a women's weight-loss lunch portion.

MEN'S OPTION No modifications.

Garlic Roasted Beets

Recipe by *Cathy Johnson*

Number of Servings: **Multiple** | Serving Size: **6 ounces** | Trigger Level: 🔔

EACH SERVING PROVIDES

VEGETABLES	FRUIT	PROTEIN	FAT	GRAIN
6 ounces	**0 ounces**	**0 serving**	**0 serving**	**0 serving**

Ingredients

5 pounds fresh beets

5 cloves fresh garlic

Olive oil spray

Pinch each of salt and black pepper

Preparation

Preheat the oven to 350°F.

Cut the greens from the beets.

Scrub the beets under running water. Peel the beets and cut them into halves. Larger beets may need to be cut into smaller pieces. All of the pieces should be about the same size so they will cook at the same rate.

Cut the garlic into thin slices.

Line a large baking sheet with parchment paper and coat it lightly with olive oil spray.

Spread the garlic evenly over the bottom of the baking sheet. Place the beets over the garlic in an even layer. Mist the tops of the beets with more oil, if desired. Season with salt and pepper.

Cover the beets and bake for 30 minutes. Check the beets; bake until they can be easily pierced with a fork.

Weigh 6 ounces for a women's weight-loss lunch portion.

MEN'S OPTION No modifications.

 Tip
If the greens are fresh looking, they can be washed and steamed in salted water, then weighed and served with the roasted beets.

Pickled Beets and Cucumbers

Recipe by *Cathy Johnson*

*"This is very reminiscent of the vinegar cukes my mother sometimes made.
I love it with or without the beets. Using beets makes a pretty
and refreshing side dish or salad."*

Number of Servings: **Multiple** | Serving Size: **6 ounces** | Trigger Level: 🔔

EACH SERVING PROVIDES

VEGETABLES	FRUIT	PROTEIN	FAT	GRAIN
6 ounces	0 ounces	0 serving	0 serving	0 serving

Ingredients

2 large cucumbers, peeled and thinly sliced

2 pounds cooked sliced beets

1 large onion, sliced into thin half rounds

1 tablespoon salt

½ cup apple cider vinegar

½ cup water

MEN'S OPTION No modifications.

Preparation

Mix all the ingredients together in a large bowl.

Add more water or vinegar as needed to cover the vegetables in the brine.

Let sit for at least 20 minutes before serving.

Weigh 6 ounces for a women's weight-loss lunch portion.

 Tip The pickled vegetables will keep in the fridge for up to 1 week.

Roasted Enchilada Vegetables

Recipe by *Erin Wallace*

Number of Servings: **Multiple** | Serving Size: **6 ounces** | Trigger Level:

EACH SERVING PROVIDES

VEGETABLES	FRUIT	PROTEIN	FAT	GRAIN
6 ounces	0 ounces	0 serving	1 serving	0 serving

Ingredients

Cooking spray

1 poblano chili, cut into matchsticks

2 red bell peppers, cut into matchsticks

½ head of cauliflower, cut into ½-inch chunks

1 large onion, sliced

1 cup frozen corn

1½ teaspoons ground cumin

1 teaspoon minced garlic

½ teaspoon sea salt

¼ teaspoon black pepper

Olive oil spray

2 cups fresh salsa (make sure sugar is not in the first 3 ingredients)

1 cup fresh baby spinach

Toppings

2 ounces diced avocado (per serving)

⅓ cup chopped fresh cilantro

MEN'S OPTION No modifications.

Preparation

Preheat the oven to 425°F. Coat a large roasting pan lightly with cooking spray.

Place the poblano, bell peppers, cauliflower, onion, and corn into a large mixing bowl. Sprinkle the cumin, garlic, salt, and pepper over the vegetables and mix together.

Spread the vegetables evenly into the prepared pan and add ¼ cup water. Roast for 40 to 50 minutes, until the vegetables are tender, stirring every 10 to 15 minutes and adding more water as necessary so the vegetables don't stick to the pan.

Remove the pan from the oven and reduce the heat to 350°F.

Coat a 9-inch square pan lightly with cooking spray. Spread ¼ cup of the salsa into the bottom of the pan, add ⅓ of the roasted vegetables, and ⅓ of the spinach.

Make two more layers of the salsa, vegetables, and spinach. Top with the remaining salsa. Cover with foil and bake for 20 minutes.

Remove the foil and bake for another 10 minutes, until the top of the casserole is lightly browned.

Let sit for 5 to 10 minutes.

Weigh 6 ounces for a women's weight-loss lunch portion.

Top with 2 ounces of diced avocado and cilantro, to taste, per serving.

Delicata Squash Rounds

Recipe by *Terry Mandel*

"These are beautiful stacked and overlapped on a platter,
whether for yourself, a potluck, or dinner guests!
Weigh your veggie portion and enjoy them, skin and all."

Number of Servings: **Multiple** | Serving Size: **6 ounces** | Trigger Level:

EACH SERVING PROVIDES				
VEGETABLES	FRUIT	PROTEIN	FAT	GRAIN
6 ounces	**0 ounces**	**0 serving**	**0 serving**	**0 serving**

Ingredients

3 delicata squash

Coconut oil spray

1 tablespoon balsamic vinegar

Preparation

Preheat the oven to 425°F.

Slice 3 uniformly shaped and similarly sized delicata squash into thick rounds.

Remove the seeds with a spoon.

Spritz a baking sheet with coconut oil spray. Place the squash rounds onto the sheet. Paint the balsamic vinegar on the top of each round with a pastry brush and bake for 8 minutes.

Turn the squash rounds over and bake for another 7 minutes before testing for doneness. The rounds are done when they can be easily pierced with a fork.

Weigh 6 ounces for a women's weight-loss lunch portion.

MEN'S OPTION No modifications.

Tip Delicata squash skins are edible and delicious.

Mexican Cauliflower Rice

Recipe by *LeeAnn Thompson*

Number of Servings: **Multiple** | Serving Size: **6 ounces** | Trigger Level: 🔔

EACH SERVING PROVIDES

VEGETABLES	FRUIT	PROTEIN	FAT	GRAIN
6 ounces	0 ounces	0 serving	1 serving	0 serving

Ingredients

20 ounces riced cauliflower

1 large yellow onion, diced

1 medium tomato, diced

6 ounces tomato paste

1 bunch fresh cilantro

4 garlic cloves, pressed

1 teaspoon salt

½ teaspoon black pepper

1 teaspoon cumin

1 teaspoon paprika

Toppings

**2 ounces diced avocado
(per serving)**

MEN'S OPTION No modifications.

Variation

→ Substitute ½ ounce chopped cashews or pistachios for the avocado.

Preparation

Add the cauliflower and onion to a deep frying pan. Add ¾ cup water (reduce to ½ cup if using frozen cauliflower rice).

Cover the pan tightly, reduce the heat to medium, and steam the vegetables until the onions are translucent.

Add the tomato, tomato paste, cilantro, garlic, and spices.

Cook uncovered over medium heat, stirring occasionally, until the extra liquid cooks off.

Weigh 6 ounces for a women's weight-loss lunch portion.

Top with 2 ounces of avocado per serving.

KAREN GRIFFIN

Before

After

The Offical **BRIGHT LINE EATING** Cookbook

134

STARTING DATE July 3, 2017
HEAVIEST WEIGHT 215 pounds
STARTING WEIGHT 193 pounds
GOAL WEIGHT ACHIEVED July 16, 2018
CURRENT WEIGHT 145 pounds
HEIGHT 5'9"

My mother and grandmother were bakers. They always made things from scratch and we indulged frequently. My mother usually baked 20 different kinds of cookies for Christmas, starting early and freezing them for the holidays. She was also famous in the family for her pie crust. My grandmother made strudels, usually apple or cherry, and we all made a special Slovenian bread called *potica*.

Still, I thought that my diet was mostly healthy, in spite of slow and steady weight gain over the years. I realize now that I had no idea what amounts of food I was consuming and often ate huge portions of the wrong things, especially when I was under stress. I used to binge on salty things, like chips, popcorn, or crackers. I didn't eat candy very often, but I could easily eat a bag of jelly beans while driving home from work. I also had ice cream and/or an alcoholic drink almost every night as a way to relax or reward myself for a busy day.

I tried many different diets and was a lifetime member of Weight Watchers in the late '80s, but was never successful after that. I just kept gaining and gaining.

With Bright Line Eating I have changed my attitude toward food. Instead of rewarding myself or decompressing with sugar, I stay within my Bright Lines. I weigh and measure everything. I enjoy my nightly gigantic salad and love having the stability of eating the same breakfast and lunch every day.

There is no doubt that BLE has changed my life. I have lost a total of 60 pounds and have never weighed this little as an adult. I am still trying to wrap my brain around this change. It is fun to feel so much better. I know that my diet is healthier. I am off almost all of my medicine, even vitamins, and just take one anti-cancer pill a day. Just amazing!

Perfect
Plates

As you're first beginning this journey, starting with meals on plates can be a helpful way to get used to the simplicity of this way of eating. Lunch is a plate with a serving of protein, a serving of vegetables (most likely with your serving of fat on them), and a piece of fruit on the side. Dinner is a serving of protein, a serving of vegetables, and a generous salad.

Laying it out like this is helpful for the first few months, and then you may find, as many of us do, that you can just dump everything into one large bowl (those are the recipes you'll find in Chapters 7 and 8). People who are on maintenance and have grains at lunch and dinner frequently enjoy having one big veggie-grain bowl with their protein of choice. Simple.

For now, allow a plate to let you start acclimating your system to what the right proportions are for a meal that will really sustain and nourish you. Let your brain form and ingrain that mental picture so that when, down the line, you are making a plate for yourself off a Thanksgiving buffet, for example, getting the right ratio of vegetables and protein will be easy.

But first we'll start by sharing some of our favorite ways to prepare protein options. Some are meat, some are vegetarian, and some are vegan. As we've said, this way of eating will work for anyone, regardless of your preferences.

PROTEINS

Susan's Tasty Tofu or Tempeh

Number of Servings: **Multiple** | Serving Size: **4 ounces** | Trigger Level: 🔔

EACH SERVING PROVIDES

VEGETABLES	FRUIT	PROTEIN	FAT	GRAIN
0 ounces	0 ounces	1 serving	0 serving	0 serving

Ingredients

One 14-ounce package extra-firm tofu

Olive oil spray

3 to 5 tablespoons soy sauce

Preparation

Dry the tofu on paper towels, pressing out as much water as possible. Then cut the tofu into ¼-inch-thick square slabs.

Coat a frying pan with olive oil spray.

Cover the bottom of the pan with a thin layer of soy sauce.

Place the tofu slabs in the pan and cook on high heat until the soy sauce has mostly evaporated (the tofu will get a little crispy).

Pour more soy sauce over the top of the tofu and turn the slabs over, cooking again until crispy.

Weigh 4 ounces tofu/tempeh for women.

MEN'S OPTION Weigh 6 ounces tofu/tempeh per serving.

Pressure-Cooked Beans

Recipe by *Julia Carol*

Number of Servings: **Multiple** | Serving Size: **6 ounces** | Trigger Level: 🔔

EACH SERVING PROVIDES

VEGETABLES	FRUIT	PROTEIN	FAT	GRAIN
0 ounces	0 ounces	1 serving	0 serving	0 serving

Ingredients

3 cups dried beans (any variety other than smaller legumes such as lentils, adzuki, and split peas)

Pinch of salt

Pinch of chili powder

Preparation

Rinse the dried beans thoroughly.

Place the beans in your pressure cooker and pour enough water over the beans until the water covers the beans by 4 inches. Let the beans soak for at least 5 hours or overnight.

Drain and rinse the beans.

Return the beans to the pressure cooker. Add enough water so that the level rises an inch above the beans.

Pressure cook the beans for 48 minutes.

Add the salt and chili powder.

Weigh 6 ounces for a women's protein serving.

Serve immediately.

MEN'S OPTION No modifications.

 Tip
You can cook the beans without soaking them first, but soaking helps reduce the gas-producing oligosaccharides and aids in digestion. You can refrigerate or freeze your cooked beans to use as entrées, or to add to soups and salads.

Quick and Juicy Chicken Breasts

Recipe by *Julia Carol*

Number of Servings: **Multiple** | Serving Size: **4 ounces** | Trigger Level: 🔔

EACH SERVING PROVIDES

VEGETABLES	FRUIT	PROTEIN	FAT	GRAIN
0 ounces	0 ounces	1 serving	0 serving	0 serving

Ingredients

Cooking spray

2 boneless, skinless chicken breasts

Pinch of garlic salt

Pinch of chili powder (optional)

Preparation

Warm a heavy skillet and coat it lightly with cooking spray.

Place the chicken breasts in the skillet. Sprinkle with a big pinch each of garlic salt and chili powder.

Cook on medium-high heat for 3 to 5 minutes, until the chicken begins to brown.

Turn the breasts over and cook for another 3 to 5 minutes, until the chicken is golden brown and cooked all the way through.

Weigh 4 ounces for a women's protein serving.

MEN'S OPTION Weigh 6 ounces of chicken per serving.

Pressure-Cooker Pulled Pork

Recipe by *Julie Boyd Smith*

*"I use this as the base for many meals, like my
pork lettuce-leaf tacos, chili, and stir-fry, or simply heated in a pan on its own!"*

Number of Servings: **Multiple** | Serving Size: **4 ounces** | Trigger Level:

EACH SERVING PROVIDES				
VEGETABLES	FRUIT	PROTEIN	FAT	GRAIN
0 ounces	0 ounces	1 serving	0 serving	0 serving

Ingredients

3 to 5 pounds bone-in pork shoulder

5 garlic cloves, peeled

4 teaspoons salt, plus more to taste

Preparation

Cut the pork into 2 or 3 pieces to fit your pressure cooker. Cut slits in the meat and insert the garlic cloves. Season the pork with the salt.

Place the pork and 1 cup water in the pressure cooker and cook on high for 90 minutes.

When the pork is cool enough to handle, separate the meat from the fat and bone.

Shred the meat.

Weigh 4 ounces for a women's protein serving.

MEN'S OPTION   Weigh 6 ounces of shredded pork per serving.

Citrus-Cilantro Shrimp

Recipe by *Sue Gaulke*

Number of Servings: **2** | Serving Size: **½ of Recipe** | Trigger Level:

EACH SERVING PROVIDES

VEGETABLES	FRUIT	PROTEIN	FAT	GRAIN
0 ounces	0 ounces	1 serving	1 serving	0 serving

Ingredients

½ ounce olive oil

½ ounce butter

1 tablespoon minced garlic

1 tablespoon lemon juice

1 tablespoon lime juice

Enough shrimp to yield
8 ounces cooked (start with
approximately 15 to 16 ounces)

2 tablespoons fresh cilantro,
chopped

½ teaspoon salt

1 teaspoon black pepper

Pinch of red pepper flakes

Preparation

Melt the oil and butter in a frying pan over medium-high heat. Add the garlic and lemon and lime juices and stir to combine.

Add the shrimp and cook until pink, about 3 to 5 minutes.

Remove pan from heat.

Using a slotted spoon, remove the shrimp from the pan and weigh out 8 ounces.

Combine the 8 ounces of shrimp with the cilantro, salt, pepper, and red pepper flakes.

Divide in half for a women's portion.

MEN'S OPTION Use same portion as women for ¾ protein and 1 fat per serving.

Grilled Salmon and Spinach Salad

Recipe by *Louanne LaRoche*

Number of Servings: **2** | Serving Size: **½ of Recipe** | Trigger Level: 🔔

EACH SERVING PROVIDES				
VEGETABLES	FRUIT	PROTEIN	FAT	GRAIN
6 ounces	0 ounces	1 serving	0 serving	0 serving

Ingredients

Olive oil spray

2 garlic cloves, thinly sliced

1 to 2 fresh salmon filets, enough to yield at least 8 ounces cooked

Salt and black pepper

1 lemon, quartered

Fresh spinach, enough to yield 12 ounces cooked

Preparation

Coat your skillet lightly with olive oil spray and set the heat to medium. Once the pan is warm, brown half of the garlic.

Season the salmon on both sides with salt and pepper.

Add the salmon to the skillet and cook to desired doneness, about 3 minutes per side.

Squeeze the juice from 2 lemon quarters over the fish; then season with more salt and pepper if desired.

Coat a separate pan with olive oil spray. Sauté the spinach and the remaining garlic until the spinach is slightly wilted. Squeeze the juice from the remaining lemon quarters and season with salt and pepper.

Weigh out 6 ounces of sautéed spinach and top with 4 ounces of salmon.

Serve immediately.

MEN'S OPTION Use 6 ounces of salmon per serving.

Cold Stuffed Pepper

Recipe by *Evelyn Zoecklein*

Number of Servings: **1** | Serving Size: **Entire Recipe** | Trigger Level: 🔔🔔

EACH SERVING PROVIDES

VEGETABLES	FRUIT	PROTEIN	FAT	GRAIN
6 ounces	0 ounces	1 serving	1 serving	0 serving

Ingredients

6 ounces red, yellow, or orange bell peppers, cut in half, seeded

4 ounces hummus, any kind you like

½ ounce pumpkin seeds

Pinch of cumin

MEN'S OPTION Use 6 ounces of hummus per serving.

Preparation

Fill the pepper halves with hummus.

Sprinkle the pumpkin seeds and cumin on top.

Herbed Blueberries with Goat Cheese

Recipe by *Julie Boyd Smith*

"I served this dish to a group of women artists
with a simple green salad (topped with oil and vinegar dressing).
Everyone thought it was wonderfully rich and indulgent,
and no one guessed it was BLE!"

Number of Servings: **1** | Serving Size: **Entire Recipe** | Trigger Level:

EACH SERVING PROVIDES

VEGETABLES	FRUIT	PROTEIN	FAT	GRAIN
0 ounces	6 ounces	1 serving	0 serving	0 serving

Ingredients

6 ounces fresh blueberries

1 ounce goat cheese

1 teaspoon fresh basil, finely diced

1 ounce sliced almonds

Preparation

Preheat the oven to 350°F.

Place half the blueberries in an ovenproof bowl. Scatter the goat cheese on top. Sprinkle the basil over; then add the remaining blueberries. Top with the almonds.

Bake at 350°F for 25 minutes or until the almonds are browned.

MEN'S OPTION Use an additional ½ ounce of goat cheese per serving.

Not Your Mom's Meatloaf

Recipe by *Ronald Mackenberg*

Number of Servings: **Multiple** | Serving Size: **5 ounces** | Trigger Level:

EACH SERVING PROVIDES

VEGETABLES	FRUIT	PROTEIN	FAT	GRAIN
1 ounce	0 ounces	1 serving	0 serving	0 serving

Ingredients

2 pounds ground beef

1 egg

8 ounces marinara sauce, divided

6 ounces riced cauliflower

2 ounces diced onion

2 teaspoons Italian herb seasoning

2 teaspoons garlic salt

Preparation

Preheat the oven to 350°F. Line a baking sheet with parchment paper.

Place the beef, egg, 4 ounces of marinara sauce, and all the remaining ingredients in a large bowl and mix by hand. Form into two loaves and place them on the baking sheet.

Bake for 40 minutes.

Top with the remaining 4 ounces of marinara sauce.

Allow to rest for 5 minutes.

Weigh a 5-ounce serving.

MEN'S OPTION Serving size is 7 ounces.

Latin Stuffed Peppers

Recipe by *Louanne LaRoche*

Number of Servings: **1** | Serving Size: **Entire Recipe** | Trigger Level:

EACH SERVING PROVIDES

VEGETABLES	FRUIT	PROTEIN	FAT	GRAIN
14 ounces	0 ounces	1 serving	1 serving	0 serving

Ingredients

10 ounces large sweet red peppers

6 ounces cooked black beans

4 ounces red onions, chopped

1 ounce cotija cheese or nondairy cheese

2 ounces salsa

1 bunch fresh cilantro, chopped

MEN'S OPTION No modifications.

Preparation

Preheat the oven to 350°F.

Slice the peppers in half and remove the seeds.

Fill each pepper half with beans and onions; then top with the cheese.

Bake the peppers for 20 minutes.

Serve topped with salsa.

Garnish with desired amount of cilantro.

Chicken Bruschetta

Recipe by *Sue Gaulke*

Number of Servings: **4** | Serving Size: **¼ Recipe** | Trigger Level: 🔔🔔

EACH SERVING PROVIDES

VEGETABLES	FRUIT	PROTEIN	FAT	GRAIN
2 ounces	0 ounces	1 serving	1 serving	0 serving

Ingredients

4 boneless, skinless chicken breasts

¼ of the Dairy-Free Pesto recipe (page 247)

2 ounces mozzarella cheese

8 ounces chopped tomatoes

Preparation

Preheat the oven to 350°F.

Bake the chicken for 10 minutes.

Turn the chicken breasts over and continue baking for 10 minutes.

Remove the chicken from the oven and weigh out four 4-ounce portions.

Evenly distribute the Dairy-Free Pesto and mozzarella cheese over the top of each portion of chicken.

Return to the oven for 5 minutes.

Remove the chicken from the oven and top each serving with 2 ounces of chopped tomatoes.

MEN'S OPTION Weigh 6 ounces of chicken for each serving.

Eggplant Parmesan

Recipe by *Ruth G. Poley*

Number of Servings: **1** | Serving Size: **Entire Recipe** | Trigger Level:

EACH SERVING PROVIDES

VEGETABLES	FRUIT	PROTEIN	FAT	GRAIN
6 ounces	0 ounces	1 serving	1 serving	0 serving

Ingredients

Olive oil spray

1 large eggplant, enough to yield 4 ounces when baked

2 ounces cooked ground beef

1 ounce shredded mozzarella cheese or nondairy cheese

1 ounce grated Parmesan or 2 ounces Nondairy Parmesan Cheese (page 230)

4 ounces marinara sauce

Pinch each of salt and black pepper

Pinch of oregano

MEN'S OPTION   Use 3 ounces of beef and 1½ ounces of mozzarella cheese per serving.

Preparation

Preheat the oven to 425°F. Coat a baking sheet lightly with olive oil spray.

Wash and peel the eggplant. Cut crosswise into 1¼- to 1½-inch-thick slices. Place the eggplant on the baking sheet and mist with olive oil spray.

Bake 15 to 20 minutes, until the eggplant softens.

Remove from oven and weigh 4 ounces of eggplant slices to be used when layering the ingredients.

Reduce the oven temperature to 350°F.

Coat a small 1- to 2-quart baking dish lightly with olive oil spray.

Place a third of the eggplant at the bottom of the baking dish. Layer with a third of the meat, a third of the mozzarella, and a third of the marinara. Season with salt, pepper, and oregano. Repeat twice more until all the ingredients are used, ending with the marinara sauce.

Top with the Parmesan, cover with foil, and bake for 30 minutes. Uncover and bake for an additional 15 minutes.

Allow to cool for 2 minutes and serve.

Variations

→ You can leave out the meat entirely and use an additional 1 ounce of cheese.

→ You can also substitute 2 ounces of crumbled tofu for the meat.

 Note 2 ounces of marinara count toward your vegetable portion and 2 ounces count toward your condiment allowance.

LISA PARROTT

Before

After

STARTING DATE **August 17, 2017**

HEAVIEST WEIGHT **310 pounds**

STARTING WEIGHT **281 pounds**

GOAL WEIGHT ACHIEVED **October 17, 2018**

CURRENT WEIGHT **161 pounds**

HEIGHT **5'10"**

*B*efore I discovered Bright Line Eating at age 44, all-consuming food thoughts had been controlling my life for decades. Sometimes the thoughts that plagued me were about specific foods—single-minded obsessions that I couldn't quiet until I had hunted down exactly what I was craving and eaten the entire bag. At other times, the thoughts were just a broad overwhelming signal screaming, "EAT. ALL. THE. FOOD. NOW!" Worst of all were the thoughts of being broken, which were accompanied by feelings of guilt and shame. I just wished I could be "normal" around food.

My eating often felt uncontrollable and relentless. I had periods of healthy eating, but I always slipped back into bingeing. I preferred to eat alone. The more overweight I became, the less I liked to eat in front of others. Social occasions became battles with myself to not eat too much of certain foods. These events usually ended with me alone at home comforting, rewarding, or punishing myself by eating.

As bleak as this life sounds, the emotional discomfort isn't what initially drove me to Bright Line Eating. My body simply couldn't support my weight any longer. Intense lower back pain made walking down a flight of stairs unbearable. I was in agony. I was also a type 2 diabetic with nonalcoholic fatty liver disease, high blood pressure, gastric reflux, sleep apnea, degenerative disk disease, and recurrent episodes of intense abdominal pain and nausea following acute gallstone pancreatitis and removal of my gallbladder. I was an addict who couldn't stop killing herself with food.

I had received a link to Susan's website from a trusted source. Thankfully that seed stayed planted in my mind until I was ready to seek help. I planned my last binge and my first day of the 14-Day Challenge at the same time. All my bases were covered!

More than 14 months later, I am still amazed by the way Bright Line Eating has allowed me to transform my old relationship with food. I have not eaten flour or sugar since Day 1. I only eat at mealtimes and I eat bounded quantities of healthy foods. I have a fifth Bright Line of No Fast Food.

My life is no longer centered on food. My food is taken care of. I don't have to worry about it anymore! And that is so humbling after decades of worry. Food feels almost effortless, to be honest, thanks to my surrender to the program, the diligent nurturing I give it every day, and my strong connection to others on this path. That is the secret to my newfound peace. I am no longer driven by my obsession or addiction. I have room to breathe. I have room to live in my new healthy body!

Chapter 7

Cold Bowls
(or Likely Lunch)

*B*right Line Eaters have a much broader definition of "salad" than most people do. We've learned we can mix cooked and chilled vegetables with raw veggies; add our protein; and then flavor with herbs, dressing, or salsa, and we've got a meal! Once veggies are prepared and waiting in the refrigerator, it's quite simple to throw together a colorful and delicious meal. We're calling these "lunch," but remember, they can easily be used for dinner if you adjust the vegetable quantities.

The key difference between Bright Line lunches and dinners on weight loss is that we have fruit at lunch, but not at dinner. If you're using one of these recipes for lunch, you need to add a fruit. If the recipe has fruit, it won't be a good option for dinner until you're on maintenance and get fruit with your dinner.

Caprese Salad

Recipe by *Ruth Martin*

*"This is one of the very first salads I ever ate on BLE.
I hadn't yet developed a taste for leafy greens, so this was as close as I got to
any kind of salad! It is still one of my favorites when I need a quick meal."*

Number of Servings: **1** | Serving Size: **Entire Recipe** | Trigger Level:

EACH SERVING PROVIDES

VEGETABLES	FRUIT	PROTEIN	FAT	GRAIN
14 ounces	0 ounces	1 serving	0 serving	0 serving

Ingredients

6 ounces cucumber, peeled and diced

6 ounces grape tomatoes, halved

2 ounces bell peppers, diced

2 ounces small mozzarella cheese curds

½ teaspoon Italian seasoning

Salt and black pepper

2 ounces balsamic vinegar

Preparation

Mix all the vegetables, mozzarella, and spices in a large bowl. If any of the mozzarella curds are bigger than bite-size pieces, you might want to cut them in half.

Drizzle with balsamic vinegar.

MEN'S OPTION Use 3 ounces of mozzarella per serving.

Simple Tuna Salad

Recipe by *Julia Carol*

Number of Servings: **1** | Serving Size: **Entire Recipe** | Trigger Level: 🔔

EACH SERVING PROVIDES

VEGETABLES	FRUIT	PROTEIN	FAT	GRAIN
0 ounces	0 ounces	1 serving	1 serving	0 servings

Ingredients

4 ounces canned tuna packed in water, drained

½ ounce mayonnaise

1 tablespoon lemon juice

1 tablespoon chopped pickles

1 teaspoon celery salt

MEN'S OPTION Use 6 ounces of tuna per serving.

Preparation

Combine the tuna, mayonnaise, and lemon juice in a small bowl.

Add the pickles and celery salt.

If more moisture is desired, add a splash of lemon juice.

Note To make a complete meal, serve over mixed greens and/or add chopped red onions and other vegetables to equal the portion for your meal.

Simple Egg Salad

Recipe by *Julia Carol*

Number of Servings: **1** | Serving Size: **Entire Recipe** | Trigger Level: 🔔

EACH SERVING PROVIDES

VEGETABLES	FRUIT	PROTEIN	FAT	GRAIN
0 ounces	0 ounces	1 serving	1 serving	0 serving

Ingredients

2 hard-boiled eggs

½ ounce mayonnaise

1 tablespoon lemon juice

Pinch each of salt and black pepper

1 tablespoon chopped pickles

1 teaspoon celery salt

MEN'S OPTION Use 3 eggs per serving.

Preparation

Mash the eggs, mayonnaise, and lemon juice together in a bowl.

Season with salt and pepper.

Add the pickles and celery salt.

Note To make a complete meal, serve over mixed greens and/or add other vegetables to equal the portion for your meal.

Quinoa and Chickpea Salad

Recipe by *Lisa Erickson*

Number of Servings: **1** | Serving Size: **Entire Recipe** | Trigger Level: 🔔

EACH SERVING PROVIDES

VEGETABLES	FRUIT	PROTEIN	FAT	GRAIN
6 ounces	0 ounces	1 serving	1 serving	0 serving

Salad Ingredients

2 ounces cooked quinoa

3 ounces cooked chickpeas

6 ounces total: chopped basil, carrots, cucumber, and tomatoes (combined)

Dressing Ingredients

½ ounce flax oil

1 tablespoon lemon juice

1 teaspoon chipotle sea salt

MEN'S OPTION No modifications.

Variation

➤ Top with 2 teaspoons of fresh basil chiffonade.

Preparation

Combine all the salad ingredients in a bowl.

Mix the oil, lemon juice, and salt in a small bowl for the dressing; then toss with the salad.

Curried Tuna Salad

Recipe by *Heidi Stallman*

*"The lemon juice and olive oil give this
tuna salad a Mediterranean flair."*

Number of Servings: **1** | Serving Size: **Entire Recipe** | Trigger Level: 🔔

EACH SERVING PROVIDES

VEGETABLES	FRUIT	PROTEIN	FAT	GRAIN
0 ounces	6 ounces	1 serving	1 serving	0 serving

Ingredients

4 ounces canned tuna packed
in water, drained

½ ounce chopped green onions

6 ounces diced Granny Smith
apple

1 teaspoon curry powder

½ ounce olive oil

1½ tablespoons lemon juice

Salt and black pepper

Preparation

Mix all the ingredients well and enjoy!

MEN'S OPTION Use 6 ounces of tuna per serving.

Variations

➤ You might also enjoy chopping celery or cucumber into this salad for crunch;
just adjust your vegetable ounces accordingly.

➤ Serve over a bed of salad greens with celery, cucumber, and carrot sticks on
the side for a full lunch vegetable portion.

➤ Use mayonnaise in place of olive oil for a more traditional tuna salad.

Grilled Shrimp with Arugula, Tomato, and Corn

Recipe by *Amy Lampert*

Number of Servings: **3** | Serving Size: **⅓ of Recipe** | Trigger Level: 🔔

EACH SERVING PROVIDES

VEGETABLES	FRUIT	PROTEIN	FAT	GRAIN
8 ounces	0 ounces	1 serving	½ serving	0 serving

Ingredients

12 ounces baby arugula

8 ounces halved cherry tomatoes

4 ounces corn, frozen and thawed or fresh

12 ounces grilled shrimp

Pinch each of salt and black pepper

½ ounce olive oil

2 tablespoons lemon juice

MEN'S OPTION Use 6 ounces of shrimp per serving.

Preparation

Toss all the ingredients together in a bowl and serve.

Crunchy Nut Butter Coleslaw

Recipe by *Kathy Lafontaine Hashley*

Number of Servings: **1** | Serving Size: **Entire Recipe** | Trigger Level: 🔔🔔🔔

EACH SERVING PROVIDES

VEGETABLES	FRUIT	PROTEIN	FAT	GRAIN
6 ounces	0 ounces	0 serving	1 serving	0 serving

Salad Ingredients

3 ounces shredded cabbage

2½ ounces carrots, grated

½ ounce green onion, sliced

Dressing Ingredients

½ ounce nut butter

¼ teaspoon liquid aminos or soy sauce

½ teaspoon lime juice

1 teaspoon rice vinegar

1½ tablespoons warm water

Pinch of cayenne pepper

Preparation

Combine the vegetables in a bowl.

Whisk together the ingredients for the dressing in a small bowl and pour over the vegetables.

Refrigerate for 2 hours before serving.

Note

This recipe is only recommended for people for whom nut butter is a neutral food. If you find after eating this that you have increased food chatter or increased cravings, either try it with a nut butter you can tolerate, or don't use this recipe.

MEN'S OPTION No modifications.

Broccoli Slaw and Roasted Corn Salad

Recipe by *Leslee Feiwus*

Number of Servings: **3** | Serving Size: **⅓ of Recipe** | Trigger Level: 🔔

EACH SERVING PROVIDES

VEGETABLES	FRUIT	PROTEIN	FAT	GRAIN
14 ounces	0 ounces	0 serving	1 serving	0 serving

Salad Ingredients

16 ounces broccoli slaw

10 ounces cherry tomatoes, halved (approximately 1 pint)

One 16-ounce bag frozen roasted corn, thawed

4½ ounces avocado

Dressing Ingredients

3 limes, juiced

4 teaspoons extra-virgin olive oil

Salt and black pepper

Preparation

Mix the lime juice, olive oil, salt, and pepper in a small bowl.

Place the broccoli slaw, cherry tomatoes, and corn in a large bowl and mix together.

When ready to eat, pour the dressing over the vegetables and toss to combine.

Divide salad into 3 equal servings.

Top each serving with 1½ ounces of avocado.

MEN'S OPTION No modifications.

Variations

→ Add 6 ounces of cooked beans or 2 ounces of feta cheese for a women's portion of protein.

→ Add 6 ounces of cooked beans or 3 ounces of feta cheese for a men's portion of protein.

Thai Nam Sod Salad

Recipe by *Evelyn Ziegler*

*"This tasty dish is on the menu in most Thai restaurants.
It contains fish sauce, a clear, salty liquid. Make sure to use the sugar-free variety;
that way it isn't sweet and won't trigger cravings."*

Number of Servings: **2** | Serving Size: **½ of Recipe** | Trigger Level:

		EACH SERVING PROVIDES		
VEGETABLES	FRUIT	PROTEIN	FAT	GRAIN
6 ounces	**6 ounces**	**1 serving**	**1 serving**	**0 serving**

Salad Ingredients

4 ounces romaine lettuce

1 ounce red onion

4 ounces red bell pepper

Thumb-sized piece of ginger root

12 ounces Granny Smith apples

1 large bunch fresh cilantro

3 ounces English cucumber

Cooking spray

Enough ground chicken, ground turkey, ground pork, or tofu to yield 8 ounces cooked

Pinch of salt

1 ounce peanuts

Dressing Ingredients

½ cup lime juice

½ cup Thai fish sauce (check that sugar is not in the first 3 ingredients)

1 teaspoon Thai garlic chili sauce

Preparation

Thinly slice the romaine lettuce, red onion, and red bell pepper lengthwise. Cut matchstick slices of raw ginger and apples. Chop the cilantro into small bite-size leaves. Slice the cucumbers into half rounds.

Coat a pan lightly with cooking spray and place over medium-high heat. Season with the salt, breaking the meat or tofu up into small bits as it cooks. Cook the ground meat until no pink remains (if using tofu, cook until it browns on all sides).

Weigh 8 ounces of ground meat or tofu into a large bowl.

Add the vegetables, ginger, apples, cilantro, and cucumbers.

To make the dressing, combine all the ingredients in a bowl and whisk.

Pour up to ½ cup dressing onto the salad—enough dressing to saturate.

Divide the salad into two equal portions.

Sprinkle each serving with ½ ounce peanuts.

MEN'S OPTION Add 2 ounces of meat or tofu per serving.

Fresh Corn and Black Bean Salad

Recipe by *LeeAnn Thompson*

Number of Servings: **1** | Serving Size: **Entire Recipe** | Trigger Level: 🔔

EACH SERVING PROVIDES				
VEGETABLES	FRUIT	PROTEIN	FAT	GRAIN
6 ounces	0 ounces	1 serving	1 serving	0 serving

Salad Ingredients

2 ounces fresh corn

2 ounces cherry tomatoes, halved

1 ounce diced peppers

1 ounce diced red onion

2 ounces cooked quinoa

3 ounces canned black beans, drained and rinsed

Dressing Ingredients

½ ounce extra-virgin olive oil

Lime juice (from ½ lime)

¼ teaspoon chili powder

Salt and black pepper

Pinch of fresh cilantro (optional)

MEN'S OPTION No modifications.

Preparation

Toss the corn, tomatoes, peppers, onion, quinoa, and beans in a bowl.

To make the dressing, whisk together the oil, lime juice, and chili powder in a small bowl. Season with salt and pepper.

Toss the salad with the dressing.

Sprinkle with cilantro, if desired, and serve.

Tip Chill the salad for an hour before serving to allow the flavors to come together.

Mediterranean Chopped Salad

Recipe by *Elaine Taylor*

Number of Servings: **1** | Serving Size: **Entire Recipe** | Trigger Level: 🔔

EACH SERVING PROVIDES

VEGETABLES	FRUIT	PROTEIN	FAT	GRAIN
8 ounces	0 ounces	1 serving	1 serving	0 serving

Salad Ingredients

6 ounces cooked chickpeas

1 lemon (zest used in salad and juice used in dressing)

Combination of the following vegetables to total 8 ounces:

- **Chopped cucumber**
- **Chopped cherry tomatoes**
- **Chopped red onion**
- **Quartered canned artichoke hearts packed in water, drained and rinsed**

½ ounce chopped Greek olives

Small handful of parsley, chopped (optional)

½ teaspoon dried oregano

Pinch each of salt and black pepper (optional)

Dressing Ingredients

⅜ ounce olive oil

½ to 1 ounce red wine or apple cider vinegar

1 tablespoon Dijon mustard

Preparation

Rinse and drain the chickpeas.

Zest the lemon.

Combine the chickpeas, lemon zest, vegetables, olives, parsley, and oregano in a large bowl. Mix well. Season with salt and pepper.

Combine the dressing ingredients in a small container. Seal with a lid and shake well to combine or whisk together.

Pour the dressing over the salad, mix well, and enjoy.

MEN'S OPTION No modifications.

Variations

- → **Women:** Substitute 1 ounce of feta cheese for 3 ounces of the chickpeas.
- → **Women:** Substitute 2 ounces of canned tuna or cooked shrimp for 3 ounces of the chickpeas.
- → **Men:** Substitute 1½ ounces of feta cheese for 3 ounces of the chickpeas.
- → **Men:** Substitute 3 ounces of canned tuna or cooked shrimp for 3 ounces of the chickpeas.

Cold Bowls (or Likely Lunch)

Sun-Dried Tomato and Kale Salad

Recipe by *Lynda Dahl*

Number of Servings: **6** | Serving Size: **⅙ of Recipe** | Trigger Level: 🔔🔔

EACH SERVING PROVIDES

VEGETABLES	FRUIT	PROTEIN	FAT	GRAIN
8 ounces	0 ounces	0 serving	⅓ serving	0 serving

Ingredients

3 ounces sun-dried tomatoes, not packed in oil

12 ounces kale

1 ounce olive oil

8 ounces carrots

11 ounces cherry or grape tomatoes (approximately 1 pint)

2 ounces red onion, chopped

6 ounces red pepper, chopped

6 ounces yellow pepper, chopped

1 lime, juiced

Balsamic vinegar, to taste

Apple cider vinegar, to taste

Pinch each of salt and black pepper

MEN'S OPTION No modifications.

Preparation

Bring a small pot of water to boil. Remove from heat.

Soak the sun-dried tomatoes in the hot water for 30 minutes, then drain and chop.

Rinse the kale leaves and remove the center stem. Chop the kale into small pieces and place in a very large bowl. (You can use a food processor to get it very finely chopped.)

Add the olive oil to the kale and massage it into the leaves using your hands.

Peel and finely shred carrots.

Add carrots, tomatoes, onion, and peppers to the kale.

Serve with the fresh lime juice, balsamic vinegar, and apple cider vinegar. Season with salt and pepper.

Tip This salad keeps in the fridge for a week.

Variation

→ Add 1⅓ ounces of guacamole to make a complete fat serving.

Chicken Fajita Bowl

Recipe by *Heidi Stallman*

*"This is a go-to meal in our house—
it's yummy and very versatile for feeding a family of non-BLE eaters."*

Number of Servings: **4** | Serving Size: **¼ of Recipe** | Trigger Level: 🔔

EACH SERVING PROVIDES				
VEGETABLES	FRUIT	PROTEIN	FAT	GRAIN
14 ounces	0 ounces	1 serving	1 serving	0 serving

Ingredients

1 ounce olive oil

3 tablespoons lime juice

3 garlic cloves, minced

1 teaspoon salt

1½ teaspoons chili powder

½ teaspoon ground cumin

1½ to 2 pounds boneless, skinless chicken thighs, cut into 1-inch strips (enough to yield 16 ounces cooked)

12 ounces white or yellow onion, sliced into strips

6 ounces red bell pepper, sliced into strips

6 ounces yellow bell pepper, sliced into strips

8 ounces lettuce

8 ounces corn

16 ounces tomatoes, chopped

4 ounces avocado, sliced

Preparation

Preheat the oven to 450°F.

Combine the olive oil, lime juice, garlic, salt, chili powder, and cumin in a large bowl.

Add the chicken, onions, and peppers and mix well. Cover and set it in the fridge for an hour to marinate, if desired, or proceed to the next step. (If you marinated the chicken and vegetables, first remove them from the marinade; then place them as described. Discard any remaining marinade.)

Set a stainless-steel rack on a rimmed baking sheet. Pour the chicken and vegetable mixture over the top of the rack and spread it out evenly in a single layer.

Place the baking sheet on the middle rack of the oven and cook for about 12 minutes. Turn the chicken and vegetables over using tongs or a metal spatula.

Cook for another 5 to 10 minutes, until the chicken and vegetables are browned. Watch carefully at this stage to make sure they do not burn.

Separate the chicken from the vegetables.

For each fajita bowl add 2 ounces of lettuce, 2 ounces of corn, and 4 ounces of tomatoes.

Top with 6 ounces of the onion and pepper mix, 4 ounces of chicken, and 1 ounce of avocado.

MEN'S OPTION Weigh 6 ounces of chicken per serving.

Variations

→ You can substitute 4 ounces of steak for the chicken thighs, but do not substitute turkey, chicken breasts, fish, or shrimp as they will get too dry during cooking with this recipe.

→ You can substitute the following:
- 3 ounces black beans for 2 ounces of chicken
- 1 ounce cheddar cheese for 2 ounces of chicken
- 1 ounce olives for 1 ounce avocado
- 1 tablespoon sour cream for 1 ounce avocado
- 2 ounces diced cucumber for 2 ounces diced tomato

→ You can add 2 ounces salsa or pico de gallo as a condiment.

→ You can also sprinkle with cilantro.

 Tip Try setting out all the salad fixings, along with traditional NMF wraps for the kids, in a buffet style so your family can make their own fajitas or salad.

Cold Bowls (or Likely Lunch)

Chicken and Apple Slaw

Recipe by *Susan Cook*

Number of Servings: **4** | Serving Size: **¼ of Recipe** | Trigger Level: 🔔

EACH SERVING PROVIDES

VEGETABLES	FRUIT	PROTEIN	FAT	GRAIN
6 ounces	6 ounces	1 serving	1 serving	0 serving

Salad Ingredients

24 ounces apples, cored and thinly sliced (approximately 4 to 6 medium apples)

½ large lemon

16 ounces cooked chicken, skinned and chopped into bite-size pieces

24 ounces precut tricolor slaw

Dressing Ingredients

2 ounces mayonnaise

2 ounces apple cider vinegar

¼ teaspoon Dijon mustard

¼ teaspoon celery salt

Preparation

Place sliced apples into a large bowl.

Squeeze the juice of the lemon over the sliced apples.

Combine the chicken and tricolor slaw with the apples.

To make the dressing, shake all the ingredients in an 8-ounce jar until mixed.

Toss the chicken apple slaw with the dressing and serve.

Tip — Use a mandolin to slice the apples. This dish refrigerates well, so you can prepare it several days in advance.

MEN'S OPTION Weigh 6 ounces of chicken per serving.

Moroccan Carrot Bowl

Recipe by *Lillian Smith*

Number of Servings: **1** | Serving Size: **Entire Recipe** | Trigger Level: 🔔

EACH SERVING PROVIDES

VEGETABLES	FRUIT	PROTEIN	FAT	GRAIN
6 ounces	0 ounces	1 serving	1 serving	0 serving

Ingredients

6 ounces cooked chickpeas

5 ounces shredded carrots

1 ounce red onion, diced

¼ teaspoon salt

½ teaspoon cumin

¼ teaspoon ground ginger

¼ teaspoon cinnamon

⅛ teaspoon coriander

⅛ teaspoon allspice

⅛ teaspoon cayenne pepper

1 lemon, juiced

½ ounce olive oil

1 garlic clove, minced

1 sprig mint or cilantro, roughly chopped

Preparation

Rinse and drain the chickpeas and place in a bowl.

Add the carrots and red onion.

Combine the salt, spices, lemon juice, olive oil, and garlic in a separate bowl and mix well.

Toss the dressing with the chickpeas and vegetables.

Top with the mint or cilantro.

MEN'S OPTION No modifications.

Texas Caviar

Recipe by *Cathy Johnson*

Number of Servings: **4** | Serving Size: **¼ of Recipe** | Trigger Level:

EACH SERVING PROVIDES

VEGETABLES	FRUIT	PROTEIN	FAT	GRAIN
6 ounces	0 ounces	1 serving	1 serving	0 serving

Ingredients

12 ounces frozen corn

16 ounces cooked black beans

8 ounces cooked black-eyed peas

2 ounces sweet onion, finely chopped

2 garlic cloves, finely chopped

2 tablespoons ground cumin

10 ounces chopped tomatoes, canned or fresh

Pinch each of salt and black pepper

2 ounces olive oil

2 ounces apple cider vinegar

½ bunch fresh cilantro, roughly chopped leaves

Preparation

Place the frozen corn in a large bowl.

Drain the black beans and black-eyed peas, rinse thoroughly, and add to the corn.

Add the onion, garlic, cumin, and tomatoes with juice. Stir together.

Sprinkle the mixture with salt and pepper; then add the oil and vinegar. Allow the mixture to sit so the corn completely defrosts and the flavors blend.

Stir in the chopped cilantro within a few hours of serving.

Season with more salt and pepper to taste.

MEN'S OPTION No modifications.

Cold Bowls (or Likely Lunch)

LAURIE AVENELL OLSON

Before

After

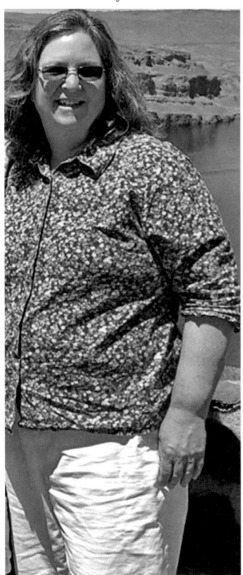

STARTING DATE **October 4, 2017**
HEAVIEST WEIGHT **245 pounds**
STARTING WEIGHT **204 pounds**
GOAL WEIGHT ACHIEVED **October 4, 2018**
CURRENT WEIGHT **146 pounds**
HEIGHT **5'5"**

I was raised with decent principles around eating. When I was young, I remember my family having three sit-down meals a day, with lots of salads, fruits, and veggies. But still, by high school, I found myself at 180 pounds. I went on the Scarsdale diet to get back down to 135, but I didn't stay there for very long.

In adulthood my weight climbed back up to 170. After having my babies, I just never could seem to lose those extra pounds. We didn't eat fast food very often, but we did eat way too many processed foods and it was very hard on my health. I had terrible headaches, stomach aches, and skin problems.

In 2010 my weight had climbed to a high of 245 pounds. I could hardly recognize myself, and thoughts of food were dominant in my life. My daughter was suffering from stomach pains, so we cut genetically engineered foods out of my family's diet. I lost 30 pounds, my husband lost 35, the kids lost 5 pounds each, and everyone felt much better. In 2011 I went gluten-free, and in 2012 we went organic. I just did not want to eat anything that had been sprayed with pesticides or herbicides.

My health improved, but I still wasn't losing the weight I wanted to lose. After experimenting with elimination diets and smoothie-only diets, in October 2017 I jumped into the BLE Boot Camp and found a community that supported me through the ups and downs of learning how to negotiate difficult situations while keeping my Bright Lines intact.

I am a solid 10 on the Susceptibility Scale, so any little slip becomes a slip and slide. Being 100 percent in is so much easier than 98 percent. At 100 percent, the food chatter in my head goes away and I find time in my life for so much more. I used to be the baker in the family; now I'm the salad maker. I don't spend hours in the kitchen anymore. I'm in and out and I've got plenty of other things to occupy my time. When things get tough, I keep my food really simple, and when things ease up, I may try something new and work it into my meal planning. Bright Line Eating has brought me so much peace around food. There is something so simple and yet so freeing about writing down what I'm going to eat each day and eating only and exactly that.

The joy I've found in the new me is well worth giving up the foods that were not doing me any favors.

Warm Bowls
(the Dinner Domain)

Warm bowls are exactly what they sound like: one vessel that holds our grain, cooked vegetables, protein, and fat. Want to make one of these recipes for lunch? Simply change the vegetable portion, grab a piece of fruit, and voilà! There are endless delicious flavor combinations. Warm bowls also include soups. One of the first questions I get asked is, "Can I still eat soup?" Absolutely! We will cover that waterfront here.

Cauliflower Fried Rice

Recipe by *Ruth Martin*

"This is one of those, 'I really don't have time for cooking tonight' recipes, as it takes about 15 minutes to put together."

Number of Servings: **3** | Serving Size: **⅓ of Recipe** | Trigger Level: 🔔

EACH SERVING PROVIDES

VEGETABLES	FRUIT	PROTEIN	FAT	GRAIN
14 ounces	0 ounces	1 serving	½ serving	0 serving

Ingredients

¾ ounce sesame oil

24 ounces frozen riced cauliflower

12 ounces frozen peas and carrots

2 garlic cloves, minced

1 tablespoon onion powder

½ to 1½ teaspoons ground ginger

6 eggs

Salt and black pepper

Preparation

Heat the sesame oil in a large frying pan.

Add the frozen cauliflower, peas and carrots, garlic, onion powder, and ginger to the pan. Cook until warmed through, approximately 8 minutes, stirring occasionally.

Scramble the eggs in a separate pan, adding salt and pepper.

Serve ⅓ of the vegetables topped with ⅓ of the scrambled eggs.

MEN'S OPTION Use 3 eggs per serving.

Variations

➤ Substitute 12 ounces of firm tofu for the eggs.

➤ Substitute the curry powder for ginger to create a slightly different flavor.

Ratatouille

Recipe by *Beth Kerrick*

Number of Servings: **Multiple** | Serving Size: **6 ounces** | Trigger Level: 🔔

EACH SERVING PROVIDES

VEGETABLES	FRUIT	PROTEIN	FAT	GRAIN
6 ounces	0 ounces	0 serving	0 serving	0 serving

Ingredients

2 medium or 3 small eggplants

4 zucchini

2 onions

3 red bell peppers

24 ounces mushrooms

8 cloves garlic

28 ounces canned tomatoes (any type)

1 tablespoon dried oregano

1 tablespoon salt

½ teaspoon black pepper

Preparation

Wash and dry all your fresh produce. Cut the eggplant and zucchini into 1-inch cubes; cut the onions and red bell peppers into 1-inch pieces. Cut the mushrooms into quarters. Finely chop the garlic.

Heat a large skillet on medium heat for 2 minutes.

Add the eggplant, zucchini, onions, peppers, mushrooms, canned tomatoes, and garlic to the skillet. Cook over medium heat until the vegetables begin to soften, about 15 minutes, stirring every 5 minutes.

Add the oregano, salt, and pepper, and cook for an additional 20 to 30 minutes or until the vegetables are soft and have released their juices. If there looks to be too much liquid at this point, drain off about a cup and discard. Cover the skillet and cook on low heat for 10 more minutes.

Serve hot or cold.

MEN'S OPTION No modifications.

 Tip To add 1 protein serving, you can pair with 6 ounces of cannellini beans or 4 ounces of cooked ground turkey or roasted chicken. To add 1 fat serving, top with 2 ounces of avocado or 1 ounce of mozzarella or nondairy cheese.

Mexican Zucchini Beef Skillet

Recipe by *Kathy Hettinger*

*"For quick weeknight meals, I make and measure the meat
and spice combination, and freeze ahead of time. Delish!"*

Number of Servings: **4** | Serving Size: **¼ of Recipe** | Trigger Level: 🔔🔔

EACH SERVING PROVIDES

VEGETABLES	FRUIT	PROTEIN	FAT	GRAIN
6 ounces	0 ounces	1 serving	1 serving	0 serving

Ingredients

**Enough ground beef (or turkey)
to yield 16 ounces cooked**

2 garlic cloves, minced

1 tablespoon chili powder

1 teaspoon ground cumin

1 teaspoon salt

½ teaspoon black pepper

½ teaspoon onion powder

¼ teaspoon crushed red pepper flakes

14 ounces zucchini, cubed

10 ounces canned crushed tomatoes

1 green chili pepper, diced

Preparation

In a large skillet, brown the ground beef over medium-high heat with the garlic and spices until cooked through.

Cook the cubed zucchini in a dry skillet over medium-high heat until browned but still firm. Add the tomatoes and green chili pepper.

Remove the beef from skillet. Weigh out 16 ounces of the beef and return it to the skillet.

Add the vegetables to the beef.

Cover and simmer for 10 minutes.

Divide into 4 equal servings and top each with 2 ounces of the diced avocado.

Toppings

8 ounces diced avocado

MEN'S OPTION Add an additional 2 ounces of beef per serving.

Variations

→ Make an Italian version with Italian spices, diced tomatoes, and marinara sauce.

→ Substitute 24 ounces canned pinto or black beans for the ground meat.

Warm Bowls (the Dinner Domain)

Hamburger and Cabbage Stir-Fry

Recipe by *Heidi Stallman*

Number of Servings: **4+** | Serving Size: **10 ounces** | Trigger Level:

EACH SERVING PROVIDES

VEGETABLES	FRUIT	PROTEIN	FAT	GRAIN
6 ounces	0 ounces	1 serving	0 serving	0 serving

Ingredients

Enough lean ground beef to yield
16 ounces cooked

1 medium onion, diced

2 cloves garlic, minced

16 ounces packaged shredded
cabbage and carrots

10 ounces peas

Salt and black pepper

1 tablespoon soy sauce (optional)

Preparation

Brown the ground beef over medium heat in a Dutch oven
or large frying pan. Remove the meat with a slotted spoon
and set aside. If there's a lot of fat still in the pan, pour most
of it off. Leave just enough to glisten the bottom of the pan.

Add the diced onion and garlic to the pan. Sauté a few
minutes until the onions are translucent.

Add the shredded cabbage and carrots to the onion and
garlic mixture. Sauté 10 to 15 minutes until the cabbage
and carrots are browned and cooked through. Sprinkle
1 teaspoon of water over the top as it is cooking if the
cabbage looks too dry.

Add the peas, cooking until they are warmed through.

Weigh 4 ounces of meat and 6 ounces of vegetables into a
bowl per serving.

Sprinkle with salt and pepper and a tablespoon of soy
sauce, if desired.

MEN'S OPTION Use 6 ounces of hamburger meat per serving.

Tip Store the meat and cabbage mixture separately,
or weigh out two more lunches for later in the
week. Throw any extra meat or veggies in with
another meal.

Italian Spaghetti Squash

Recipe by *Ellen Eichen Weinman*

Number of Servings: **1** | Serving Size: **15 ounces** | Trigger Level: 🔔🔔

EACH SERVING PROVIDES

VEGETABLES	FRUIT	PROTEIN	FAT	GRAIN
6 ounces	0 ounces	1 serving	1 serving	0 serving

Ingredients

Cooking spray

1 large spaghetti squash

2 teaspoons salt

1 teaspoon freshly ground black pepper

2 teaspoons fennel seeds

1 tablespoon parsley flakes

2 teaspoons oregano

1 teaspoon garlic powder

2 ounces spaghetti sauce (check that sugar is not in the first 3 ingredients)

6 ounces beans

1 ounce Parmesan cheese

MEN'S OPTION No modifications.

Preparation

Preheat oven to 400°F. Coat a baking pan lightly with cooking spray.

Slice the squash in half; scoop out and discard the seeds. Place the squash cut side down on the tray and bake for 30 minutes.

Let cool; then use a fork to scrape out the strands of squash.

Place 6 ounces of cooked spaghetti squash in a pot and mix with all the seasonings.

Add 2 ounces of spaghetti sauce and 6 ounces beans and heat through over medium heat.

Sprinkle with 1 ounce cheese and serve.

Coconut Curry Stir-Fry

Recipe by *Julia Harold*

Number of Servings: **1** | Serving Size: **Entire Recipe** | Trigger Level: 🔔

EACH SERVING PROVIDES

VEGETABLES	FRUIT	PROTEIN	FAT	GRAIN
14 ounces	0 ounces	1 serving	1 serving	0 serving

Ingredients

4 ounces extra-firm tofu

2 ounces red Thai curry paste

Coconut oil cooking spray

Enough combined stir-fry vegetables to yield 14 ounces cooked:

- onions, carrots, zucchini, broccoli
- onions, brussels sprouts, cubed butternut squash
- onions, bok choy, carrots, snow peas, bell pepper, mushrooms

2 ounces canned coconut milk

Preparation

Cut the tofu into cubes.

Mix the curry paste with ½ cup water in a bowl.

Preheat a large pan over medium-high heat.

Lightly coat the pan with cooking spray and sauté the onions until translucent.

Add the remaining vegetables and sauté for another 1 to 2 minutes.

Add the curry paste mixture and tofu; then immediately cover the pan.

Cook until the vegetables are done to your liking, adding more water if the pan becomes dry.

Transfer the contents of the pan to a single-serving bowl.

Add 2 ounces of coconut milk, stir, and enjoy.

MEN'S OPTION Use 6 ounces of tofu per serving.

Variation

→ Substitute green Thai curry paste for red for a different flavor.

Steamed Kale and Lentil Bowl

Recipe by *Evelyn Zoecklein*

Number of Servings: **1** | Serving Size: **Entire Recipe** | Trigger Level: 🔔🔔

EACH SERVING PROVIDES

VEGETABLES	FRUIT	PROTEIN	FAT	GRAIN
6 ounces	6 ounces	1 serving	1 serving	0 serving

Ingredients

6 ounces steamed kale

6 ounces grapefruit sections, chopped

3 ounces cooked lentils

2 ounces feta cheese or nondairy cheese, crumbled

Pinch of cinnamon

Preparation

Mix all the ingredients together.

Sprinkle the cinnamon on top.

MEN'S OPTION Use 2½ ounces of feta cheese per serving.

Note This recipe uses feta cheese as 1 fat serving and ½ protein serving.

SOUPS & STEWS

Measuring soup is tricky. It typically contains a mixture of food categories, such as protein and vegetables, and possibly grains, too (for example, barley beef soup with vegetables). Plus, there's all the broth. This makes it really hard to weigh.

For this reason, I personally don't eat soup at home. I do, however, eat lentil soup or vegetarian chili if I'm out at a restaurant, and count it for my protein serving. Typically, I just use the bowl as my measurement and eat what they serve me.

But if you are someone who absolutely *loves* soup and would be heartbroken not to be able to eat it at home, don't despair. Just because I don't eat it doesn't mean you can't. A lot of Bright Lifers live on soups and stews during colder weather. You'll just have to plan ahead and do some creative math.

And remember, the main point of weighing our food is not because our body really cares whether we get 14 ounces of vegetables or 13 or 15 ounces, it's because our brains need to relax into the consistency of knowing we've gotten enough. It puts a boundary around the meal, and ultimately respecting that boundary becomes automatic and we find ourselves living Happy, Thin, and Free. The good news about making soup at home is that once you have your way of cooking it and your way of measuring it, turning that recipe into a meal can become as automatic as weighing 6 ounces of blueberries or 8 ounces of yogurt.

In general, a serving of soup that is both a protein serving and a vegetable serving would be 12 ounces if the broth is thick, or 14 ounces if the broth is on the thin side.

For soups that are broth based (in other words, very thin), you may strain the vegetable and/or protein content, and then weigh according to your food plan portions. Add 8 ounces of broth back in afterward.

Don't panic—as with everything else, you will get the hang of it and it will become automatic.

African Bean Stew

Recipe by *Chef Katie Mae,* TheCulinaryGym.com

*"This is a rich stew with complex flavors.
I often use it when I'm having company."*

Number of Servings: **3** | Serving Size: **⅓ of Recipe** | Trigger Level:

EACH SERVING PROVIDES				
VEGETABLES	FRUIT	PROTEIN	FAT	GRAIN
14 ounces	0 ounces	1 serving	1 serving	0 serving

Ingredients

4 ounces onion, diced (1 small)

1 to 2 tablespoons jalapeño, seeded and minced

8 ounces cauliflower, chopped (½ medium head)

20 ounces chopped tomatoes

3 tablespoons peanut or almond butter, unsweetened

½ tablespoon ground ginger

½ tablespoon ground coriander

½ tablespoon garlic granules

6 ounces collard or kale, sliced in ribbons (1 bunch)

9 ounces chickpeas (1½ cups, 15-ounce can, drained and rinsed)

9 ounces black-eyed peas, (1½ cups, 15-ounce can, drained and rinsed)

6 ounces frozen peas or corn, thawed

3 ounces red bell pepper, diced (1 medium)

½ to 1 lemon, juiced

MEN'S OPTION No modifications.

Preparation

Place the onion, jalapeño, and cauliflower in a large pot over medium heat. Cover and dry-sauté the veggies, until the onions soften, stirring frequently to prevent sticking.

Add the tomatoes, 1 cup water, nut butter, ginger, coriander, and garlic granules. Bring to a boil and then turn the heat to medium; let the soup simmer for 10 minutes.

Stir in the collards, let them soften for a few minutes, and then stir in the chickpeas, black-eyed peas, peas, and bell pepper. Continue simmering until everything is warmed through and the collards are bright green and tender. Remove from the heat and serve with a squeeze of lemon.

Nonie Evie's Tomato Soup

Recipe by *Evelyn Zoecklein*

*"This is an old family recipe that my grandmother used to make.
It was especially comforting when we weren't feeling well."*

Number of Servings: **1** | Serving Size: **Entire Recipe** | Trigger Level: 🔔

EACH SERVING PROVIDES

VEGETABLES	FRUIT	PROTEIN	FAT	GRAIN
14 ounces	0 ounces	1 serving	1 serving	0 serving

Ingredients

14 ounces diced tomatoes

½ teaspoon baking soda

8 ounces milk

**½ ounce unsalted butter
or olive oil**

Pinch of ground black pepper

MEN'S OPTION No modifications.

Preparation

Cook the tomatoes in a saucepan over medium-high heat until broken down, about 8 minutes.

Reduce the heat to low and add the baking soda and milk, being careful not to let boil.

Once the mixture is hot, add the butter and ground pepper, and serve.

"Cream" of Broccoli Soup

Recipe by *C.J. Hast*

Number of Servings: **1** | Serving Size: **Entire Recipe** | Trigger Level: 🔔🔔

EACH SERVING PROVIDES

VEGETABLES	FRUIT	PROTEIN	FAT	GRAIN
14 ounces	0 ounces	1 serving	1 serving	0 serving

Ingredients

14 ounces steamed broccoli (save the water)

1½ ounces walnuts

½ teaspoon salt

1 hard-boiled egg or 2 ounces firm tofu

Preparation

Add the steamed broccoli, walnuts, salt, and broccoli water to a blender and blend to desired consistency. Add more or less broccoli water to reach desired thickness.

Top with the sliced hard-boiled egg or crumbled tofu and serve.

MEN'S OPTION Use 2 hard-boiled eggs or 4 ounces firm tofu per serving.

Note While we do not make smoothies on Bright Line Eating, many of us are able to have blended soups like this without any issue. Half of the protein serving in this recipe comes from 1 ounce of the walnuts and the remaining ½ ounce of walnuts provides the fat serving.

Chipotle Vegan Sausage and White Bean Stew

Recipe by *Lisa Branic*

Number of Servings: **3** | Serving Size: **⅓ of Recipe** | Trigger Level:

EACH SERVING PROVIDES

VEGETABLES	FRUIT	PROTEIN	FAT	GRAIN
6 ounces	0 ounces	1 serving	0 serving	0 serving

Ingredients

1½ teaspoons minced garlic

⅛ teaspoon crushed red pepper flakes

One 15½-ounce can fire-roasted diced tomatoes

12 ounces vegetable broth

One 5½-ounce bag washed spinach leaves or freshly washed spinach

9 ounces white cannellini beans, drained and rinsed

6 ounces vegan sausage (such as Field Roast Mexican chipotle sausage), cut into ¼-inch rounds

Preparation

Place the garlic, red pepper flakes, and 1 tablespoon of water in a saucepan over medium heat and sauté until the garlic is golden brown, about 1 minute. Add the tomatoes and broth and bring to a boil.

Add the spinach. Cook until the spinach is wilted.

Heat beans and sausage in separate pans.

Divide the contents of the saucepan into three soup bowls.

Add 3 ounces of heated beans and 2 ounces of heated sausage to each bowl.

 Note In Bright Line Eating, up to 8 ounces of vegetable broth is considered a condiment. This recipe uses 4 ounces per serving.

MEN'S OPTION Use 3 ounces of beans and 3 ounces of vegan sausage per serving.

Lamb Stew

Recipe by *Louanne LaRoche*

Number of Servings: **2** | Serving Size: **½ of Recipe** | Trigger Level:

EACH SERVING PROVIDES				
VEGETABLES	FRUIT	PROTEIN	FAT	GRAIN
14 ounces	0 ounces	1 serving	¼ serving	0 serving

Ingredients

12 ounces eggplant, cut into bite-size pieces

12 ounces fire-roasted tomatoes

6 ounces mirepoix (diced onion, carrots, and celery)

1 ounce Kalamata olives, pitted

Handful of fresh cilantro, chopped

1 teaspoon curry powder

Enough lean lamb, cubed, to yield 8 ounces cooked

Preparation

Place the eggplant, tomatoes, mirepoix, olives, cilantro, and curry in a Dutch oven and cook over medium heat until the eggplant is tender, about 25 minutes.

Add the lamb and cook until the meat is cooked through, about 20 minutes.

Divide into two equal servings and enjoy.

MEN'S OPTION Use 6 ounces of lamb per serving.

White Bean and Pumpkin Soup

Recipe by *Julia Carol*

Number of Servings: **3+** | Serving Size: **16 ounces** | Trigger Level: 🔔

EACH SERVING PROVIDES

VEGETABLES	FRUIT	PROTEIN	FAT	GRAIN
10 ounces	0 ounces	1 serving	1 serving	0 serving

Ingredients

6 ounces carrots, diced

6 ounces red onion, diced

4½ ounces celery, diced

4 cups low-sodium vegetable broth

15 ounces unsweetened pumpkin puree

1 tablespoon garlic granules

2 bay leaves

½ tablespoon dried sage

½ tablespoon dried rosemary

6 ounces curly kale, chopped (about 1 bunch, stems removed)

18 ounces cooked great northern beans

Toppings

2 ounces avocado, diced, per serving

Preparation

Place the carrots, onion, and celery in a large pot over medium heat. Cover and cook until the onions start to become translucent, stirring occasionally so the vegetables do not stick.

Add the broth, pumpkin, garlic, and herbs. Bring the liquid to a boil, then reduce the heat to low.

Simmer uncovered for 10 minutes. The soup will thicken as it cooks.

Add the kale. Continue cooking until the kale is tender and the soup reaches your desired consistency.

Remove the bay leaves.

Heat beans in a separate pan.

For each serving, weigh 10 ounces of soup into a bowl and add 6 ounces of beans.

Top each serving with 2 ounces diced avocado.

MEN'S OPTION No modifications.

Chicken and Vegetable Soup

Recipe by *Heidi Stallman*

Number of Servings: **Multiple** | Serving Size: **18 ounces** | Trigger Level: 🔔

EACH SERVING PROVIDES

VEGETABLES	FRUIT	PROTEIN	FAT	GRAIN
6 ounces	0 ounces	1 serving	0 serving	0 serving

Ingredients

Olive oil spray

2½ pounds boneless, skinless chicken thighs

Pinch of salt

1 large onion, diced

5 celery stalks, chopped

4 carrots, chopped

1 medium zucchini, chopped

3 bay leaves

1 teaspoon black pepper

4 to 6 cups chicken broth

8 ounces chopped kale (optional)

Preparation

Coat the bottom of a soup pot with olive oil spray and add the chicken thighs. Sprinkle with salt and cook over medium heat until lightly browned, about 10 minutes, turning once.

Add the onion, celery, carrots, zucchini, bay leaves, and pepper. Sauté with the chicken for about 5 minutes, until the onions are translucent.

Add the broth and let simmer for about 30 minutes, until the vegetables are starting to soften.

Add the kale, if using. Cook for another 10 to 15 minutes, until the vegetables and chicken are cooked through.

Transfer the chicken to a plate using a slotted spoon. Chop into bite-size pieces.

For each serving, use a slotted spoon and weigh 6 ounces of vegetables into a bowl.

Add 8 ounces of the broth and 4 ounces of chicken to each bowl.

MEN'S OPTION Weigh 6 ounces of chicken per serving.

Tip Store the meat in a separate container than the vegetables and broth for easy portion measurement.

Very Veggie Chili

Recipe by *Susan Gilbert Zencka*

Number of Servings: **5+** | Serving Size: **21 ounces** | Trigger Level: 🔔

EACH SERVING PROVIDES

VEGETABLES	FRUIT	PROTEIN	FAT	GRAIN
14 ounces	0 ounces	1 serving	1 serving	0 serving

Ingredients

Cooking spray

1 large onion, chopped

1 pepper (red, green, yellow, or orange), chopped

½ cup mushrooms, chopped

Two 24-ounce cans crushed tomatoes

1 zucchini, chopped

1 yellow squash, chopped

⅓ head cauliflower, chopped

1 large carrot, chopped

1 cup corn

1 to 2 jalapeños, finely chopped (optional)

2 tablespoons cumin

1 tablespoon medium chili powder

Pinch of chipotle powder

1 teaspoon cinnamon

½ teaspoon cloves

½ teaspoon allspice

10 ounces cooked black beans

10 ounces cooked pinto beans

10 ounces cooked red kidney beans

5 ounces tofu sour cream

Preparation

Mist a large skillet with cooking spray and sauté the onions and peppers over medium-high heat.

Add the remaining ingredients, except the beans and tofu sour cream, and simmer for 45 minutes.

Heat the beans in a small pot over medium heat. When hot, drain.

Weigh 14 ounces of the vegetable mixture and add 6 ounces of beans.

Garnish with 1 ounce of tofu sour cream per serving.

MEN'S OPTION No modifications.

Variation

→ Substitute 2 ounces avocado or ½ ounce sesame seeds for 1 ounce of tofu sour cream, per serving.

LINDA SCHMITZ

Before

After

STARTING DATE   **March 5, 2018**
HEAVIEST WEIGHT   **247 pounds**
STARTING WEIGHT   **227 pounds**
GOAL WEIGHT ACHIEVED   **November 8, 2018**
CURRENT WEIGHT   **148 pounds**
HEIGHT   **5'7"**

*E*ver since high school, I can't remember any long stretch of time when I wasn't focusing energy on what I was eating or, frankly, what I *wasn't* eating. Food was always on my mind in one way or another. I would go through periods of successful management of my food only to be followed by regaining the weight I'd lost after reverting to unhealthy food choices. I remember that when I was pregnant with my daughter, I had successfully given up many unhealthy foods, including artificial sweeteners, but after she was born I immediately requested a Diet Coke to be brought into our hospital room. Looking back, what seemed quirky was just another symptom of my long struggle.

I considered myself a true "foodie." I would plan vacations around food options and would often Yelp restaurants before I even booked a hotel! I would even pack my favorite sweetened beverage in my suitcase in case I couldn't find it when we arrived. Looking back at vacation photos, a good portion of them revolve around restaurants and what we ate, rather than on the adventures themselves. Ultimately, this led me to being more than 100 pounds overweight in my early 30s.

Fast-forward to where I am today: full of energy and fueling my body with large amounts of healthy and delicious food every day. While delicious, food is no longer a focus, but rather just another way I take care of myself. Once my taste buds got unaccustomed to the Standard American Diet, real food now tastes amazing and I no longer have cravings for unhealthy foods. Rather than feeling deprived, I truly appreciate the wonderful tasty food I am using to fuel my body.

Part of me wishes that I was a person who could eat anything in moderation, but I know the journey I have traveled. If I had not had my struggles, there is no way I would be making such healthy food choices day in and day out.

Dressings, Sauces, and Salsas

There are those Bright Line Eaters who have almost the same meal day after day and find themselves loving it so much that there's no need for variation. Then there are many Bright Line Eaters who eat similar meals but get their variety from using different dressings, sauces, or salsas.

We've learned that not all delicious salad dressing has to have fat, that nuts ground and blended in a high-speed mixer with liquid add a creamy texture, and herbs and spices are our friends. Here are some of our Bright Lifer favorites. Enjoy!

Nondairy Parmesan Cheese

Recipe by *Julia Carol*

Number of Servings: **8** | Serving Size: **⅛ of Recipe** | Trigger Level: 🔔🔔🔔

EACH SERVING PROVIDES

VEGETABLES	FRUIT	PROTEIN	FAT	GRAIN
0 ounces	0 ounces	0 servings	1 serving	0 serving

Ingredients

4 ounces walnuts

1 cup nutritional yeast

1 teaspoon salt

1 teaspoon garlic salt

1 teaspoon paprika

MEN'S OPTION No modifications.

Preparation

Finely chop the walnuts.

Blend all the ingredients in a high-speed blender.

Refrigerate.

Balsamic Vinaigrette

Recipe by *Vicki Weik*

*"This is an absolutely fabulous-tasting salad dressing.
I bring it with me whenever I will be having a salad!"*

Number of Servings: **Multiple** | Serving Size: **2 tablespoons** | Trigger Level: 🔔

EACH SERVING PROVIDES

VEGETABLES	FRUIT	PROTEIN	FAT	GRAIN
0 ounces	0 ounces	0 serving	1 serving	0 serving

Ingredients

½ cup balsamic vinegar

2 tablespoons Dijon mustard

2 tablespoons garlic paste

1 teaspoon salt

1 teaspoon black pepper

⅓ cup toasted organic sesame oil

⅓ cup walnut, flax, or avocado oil

MEN'S OPTION No modifications.

Preparation

Combine all the ingredients, except the oils, and mix together.

Combine the sesame and walnut oils in a separate bowl.

Slowly add the oils to the vinegar mixture, whisking to emulsify the dressing.

Lemon Tahini Dressing

Recipe by *Teri Meggers*

*"This dressing lends itself well
to the addition of many herbs and spices."*

Number of Servings: **4** | Serving Size: **1 ounce** | Trigger Level: 🔔

EACH SERVING PROVIDES

VEGETABLES	FRUIT	PROTEIN	FAT	GRAIN
0 ounces	0 ounces	0 serving	1 serving	0 serving

Ingredients

2 ounces tahini

2 ounces fresh lemon juice

MEN'S OPTION No modifications.

Variation

➤ You can add mustard, salsa, dill, turmeric, or your favorite herb.

Preparation

Whisk tahini and lemon juice together until well mixed.

Add 1 tablespoon of water to the dressing if you prefer a thinner consistency.

Tip Keep individual servings in the fridge for dressing on the go.

Hummus Dressing

Recipe by *Julia Harold*

*"I never get tired of this dressing.
The ume plum vinegar is what makes it so good."*

Number of Servings: **1** | Serving Size: **Entire Recipe** | Trigger Level: 🔔

EACH SERVING PROVIDES

VEGETABLES	FRUIT	PROTEIN	FAT	GRAIN
0 ounces	0 ounces	0 serving	1 serving	0 serving

Ingredients

2 ounces hummus

¼ ounce ume plum vinegar

¼ ounce balsamic vinegar

Preparation

Place all the ingredients in a small bowl.

Whisk the ingredients vigorously until mixed thoroughly.

MEN'S OPTION No modifications.

Variation

➤ Use 4 ounces of hummus instead of 2 ounces. Count this as your protein rather than your fat. The creaminess goes a long way on a large salad.

Southwest-Style Vinaigrette

Recipe by *Heidi Stallman*

*"This dressing is especially good on a
Southwest-style bean salad."*

Number of Servings: **1** | Serving Size: **Entire Recipe** | Trigger Level: 🔔

EACH SERVING PROVIDES

VEGETABLES	FRUIT	PROTEIN	FAT	GRAIN
0 ounces	0 ounces	0 serving	1 serving	0 serving

Ingredients

½ ounce olive oil

½ ounce apple cider vinegar

½ teaspoon cumin

¼ teaspoon chili powder

1 garlic clove, minced

Pinch each of salt and black pepper

Preparation

Mix all the ingredients in a small bowl.

MEN'S OPTION No modifications.

Variations

➤   Substitute red wine vinegar for the apple cider vinegar.

➤   You can also add extra vinegar or spices depending on your taste.

Miso Tahini Dressing

Recipe by *Mary Mazzone*

Number of Servings: **Multiple** | Serving Size: **2 ounces** | Trigger Level: 🔔

EACH SERVING PROVIDES				
VEGETABLES	FRUIT	PROTEIN	FAT	GRAIN
0 ounces	0 ounces	0 serving	1 serving	0 serving

Ingredients

¼ cup white miso

¼ cup unsweetened, unsalted sesame tahini

¼ cup Dijon mustard

¼ cup apple cider vinegar

Preparation

Blend all the ingredients together in a high-speed blender.

Serve 2 ounces as your fat portion.

MEN'S OPTION No modifications.

Variation

➤ You can substitute balsamic vinegar for the apple cider vinegar.

Guacamole Sauce

Recipe by *Lynda Dahl*

Number of Servings: **Multiple** | Serving Size: **2 ounces** | Trigger Level: 🔔

EACH SERVING PROVIDES				
VEGETABLES	FRUIT	PROTEIN	FAT	GRAIN
0 ounces	0 ounces	0 serving	1 serving	0 serving

Ingredients

3 peeled, pitted avocados

⅓ cup chopped onion

⅓ cup cilantro

3 tablespoons lemon juice

½ teaspoon salt

3 teaspoons chili powder

MEN'S OPTION No modifications.

Preparation

Blend all the ingredients in a high-speed food processor until combined and smooth in consistency.

Serve 2 ounces as your fat portion.

Tip

If you do not have food processor, you can combine this sauce in a bowl with a spoon.

Roasted Red Pepper and Almond Sauce

Recipe by *Lisa Branic*

"This sauce is delicious.
You can pour it over veggies, tofu, chicken, or an omelet.
It's a lot of sauce for just one fat serving!"

Number of Servings: **4** | Serving Size: **¼ of Recipe** | Trigger Level: 🔔

EACH SERVING PROVIDES

VEGETABLES	FRUIT	PROTEIN	FAT	GRAIN
2 ounces	0 ounces	0 serving	1 serving	0 serving

Ingredients

One 15-ounce jar roasted red peppers (or 3 roasted red peppers)

2 ounces slivered almonds

2 garlic cloves, peeled and crushed

¼ cup lemon juice

1 teaspoon dried thyme

Pinch of salt

MEN'S OPTION No modifications.

Preparation

Blend all the ingredients in a high-speed blender.

Fresh Salsa with Ginger

Recipe by *Erin Wallace*

Number of Servings: **Multiple** | Serving Size: **2 ounces** | Trigger Level: 🔔

EACH SERVING PROVIDES

VEGETABLES	FRUIT	PROTEIN	FAT	GRAIN
0 ounces	0 ounces	0 serving	0 serving	0 serving

Ingredients

6 vine-ripened tomatoes, seeded and chopped

½ medium red onion, finely chopped

1-inch piece ginger root, peeled and finely chopped

2 jalapeños, finely chopped

1 tablespoon fresh lime juice

½ teaspoon salt

⅛ teaspoon black pepper

MEN'S OPTION No modifications.

Preparation

Stir all the ingredients together.

Chill for at least 1 hour before serving.

Note Two ounces of this is a condiment. You can use more and count it as part of your vegetable serving.

Basil-Lemon Dressing

Recipe by *Susan Gilbert Zencka*

Number of Servings: **1** | Serving Size: **Entire Recipe** | Trigger Level: 🔔🔔🔔

EACH SERVING PROVIDES

VEGETABLES	FRUIT	PROTEIN	FAT	GRAIN
0 ounces	0 ounces	1 serving	0 serving	0 serving

Ingredients

4 ounces almond milk

1 ounce raw cashews

1 tablespoon grainy mustard

¼ cup lemon juice

1 large handful basil

2 garlic cloves

MEN'S OPTION No modifications.

Preparation

Blend all the ingredients in a high-speed blender.

Dairy-Free Pesto

Recipe by *Susan Cook*

Number of Servings: **Multiple** | Serving Size: **1 ounce** | Trigger Level: 🔔🔔

EACH SERVING PROVIDES

VEGETABLES	FRUIT	PROTEIN	FAT	GRAIN
0 ounces	0 ounces	0 serving	1 serving	0 serving

Ingredients

1½ cups fresh basil leaves

2 ounces raw almonds, toasted

2 tablespoons nutritional yeast

2 ounces olive oil or avocado oil

MEN'S OPTION No modifications.

Preparation

Blend all the ingredients and 2 tablespoons water in a food processor until smooth.

Peppers and Tomato Sauce

Recipe by *Leslee Feiwus*

Number of Servings: **Multiple** | Serving Size: **2 ounces** | Trigger Level: 🔔

EACH SERVING PROVIDES

VEGETABLES	FRUIT	PROTEIN	FAT	GRAIN
0 ounces	0 ounces	0 serving	0 serving	0 serving

Ingredients

6 Roma tomatoes, halved

8 small tomatillos, halved

1 yellow onion, chopped

One 1-pound bag small yellow, orange, and red peppers, seeded and halved

4 garlic cloves

Cooking spray

Pinch each of salt and black pepper

1 bunch cilantro

1 lime, juiced

MEN'S OPTION No modifications.

Preparation

Preheat the oven to 400°F.

Place the tomatoes, tomatillos, onion, peppers, and garlic on a baking sheet and lightly spray with cooking spray. Season with salt and pepper.

Roast for 1 hour.

Transfer the roasted vegetables to a mixing bowl and add the cilantro and lime juice. Blend with an immersion blender. If you don't have an immersion blender, allow the vegetables to cool and then blend in a high-speed blender or food processor.

Note Two ounces of this is a condiment. You can use more and count it as part of your vegetable serving.

Creole Sauce

Recipe by *Ellen Eichen Weinman*

*"This sauce is so good over
vegetables, meatballs, chicken, or pork."*

Number of Servings: **4** | Serving Size: **¼ of Recipe** | Trigger Level: 🔔

EACH SERVING PROVIDES

VEGETABLES	FRUIT	PROTEIN	FAT	GRAIN
6 ounces	0 ounces	0 serving	½ serving	0 serving

Ingredients

1 ounce butter

3 ounces finely chopped green pepper

2 ounces finely chopped onion

1 garlic clove, crushed

One 15-ounce can tomato puree

One 3-ounce can sliced mushrooms, including liquid

MEN'S OPTION No modifications.

Preparation

Melt the butter in a medium saucepan over high heat.

Add the pepper, onion, and garlic, and cook until the vegetables soften.

Reduce the heat to low and stir in the tomato puree and mushrooms.

Simmer gently for 25 to 30 minutes.

LOUANNE LAROCHE

Before

After

STARTING DATE **March 1, 2016**
HEAVIEST WEIGHT **352 pounds**
STARTING WEIGHT **338 pounds**
GOAL WEIGHT ACHIEVED **August 17, 2018**
CURRENT WEIGHT **177 pounds**
HEIGHT **5'6"**

*S*ince early childhood I have had a love-hate relationship with food. Foods I associated with special events or rewards became comfort food when I didn't know how to handle emotions or situations. Flour, sugar, and fat in any form, including raw, quickly became my drugs of choice, and I would go to any lengths to get them. Healthy food was not celebrated. I knew I was destroying my body, health, mind, and spirit, but I could not stop.

I am an artist, so color stimulates my brain. Now that my brain is healing, it naturally gravitates to healthy foods. Fresh vegetables and fruits displayed in farmers' markets now turn me on. Once flour and sugar were out of my system, all my senses reawakened, and my Bright Line meals beautifully displayed on my plate are very satisfying.

Monday morning my fridge is loaded with greens and vegetables of all colors.

I also prepare meals in advance so when I am on the go or have had a long day I don't suffer from my diminished reserves. My affirmation is "I am what I eat. Fresh, Beautiful, and Healthy."

My early Girl Scouts training of being prepared has served me well. I plan, plan, and plan some more so that I have what I need and extra for emergencies. I bring extra weighed and measured food to functions or restaurants or as a contribution to a group meal. When I take care of myself, I am free to really connect and be present with others. Usually, my selections are envied by others and I am empowered by my willingness to overcome what others may see as challenges. Planning minimizes stress and poor food choices.

Now I go to any lengths to maintain my success, by using the tools of keeping a food journal, committing my weighed and measured food, connecting with others in the Bright Line community, and celebrating every day by sitting down to eat my nurturing Bright Line meals, one day at a time.

Chapter 10

Tips, Tricks, and Techniques from Bright Lifers

I asked some of our Bright Lifers to share with us their best tips, tricks, and techniques for making sure they always have Bright Line meals available. In sharing this hard-won wisdom, our community is inviting you to take a peek into our way of life. Come and see how our healed brains organize around food. We hope you'll find some of these nuggets useful, and others may inspire you to create your own methods.

Some tips are specific to prepping a certain food, but most involve ways to be sure we'll have our food ready when it's time to eat. We include ideas on how to travel successfully, as well as planning for meals at home.

My own best tip to you? It's simple but powerful: Plan. Yup, *plan*. As the saying goes, if you fail to plan, you plan to fail. The easiest path to a peaceful brain and automaticity around food is to eliminate food choices made "in the moment" and have your food ready in advance.

FOOD PREP

When eating at home, Bright Lifers find preparing large batches of food for the week to be helpful as well as economical for their wallets and schedules. If you spend a few hours once or twice a week doing the shopping and chopping, the rest falls into place, and meal prep becomes simple. As Bright Lifer Julia Carol puts it, "I get a big grin and feel my body relax when I open the refrigerator to find neatly stacked containers with all the veggies and protein I'll need for a few days in a row. I feel held and safe and happy."

We all develop our own habits in order to accomplish prebatched food. In warmer weather, we might chop all our fresh vegetables (minus greens) and keep them together in one large container, and then add the correct quantity to our greens and protein and fat for a big bowl of salad.

In colder weather, batch cooking may mean making a huge pot of soup or stew for many meals in advance; or roasting, steaming, or sautéing several days' worth of vegetables to reheat quickly at mealtime.

"I take a piece of graph paper, oriented landscape, and write
B (breakfast) L (lunch) D (dinner) evenly spaced down the left side.
Across, I write the days of the week. I shop twice a week. On the far
right, I write Grocery List. I plan each meal, listing all the components."

— *Molly Doogan*

"I could not do BLE without my meal plan shopping list.
One day a week I will plan out my meals for the upcoming week.
Using my pantry, fridge, and freezer I check to see what I have on hand.
From this I make my shopping list. Shopping is much easier now."

— *Lynn Powers*

"My weeks are ALWAYS busy, so planning is the key for me. I can't
tell you the number of times I grab my meal from the freezer because
my plans have changed, and I need to GO! Glass seems to keep food
longest, so I use a lot of Ball jars in both the refrigerator and freezer."

— *Julie Boyd Smith*

"I make steel-cut oats to last for four to five days. Each morning, I measure out the cooked oats, add a little water, mix, and heat in the microwave. Then I add my correct quantities of fruit, nuts and seeds for protein, and spices. I also make enough beans in the pressure cooker to last for four to five days. Then I just have to reheat my measured serving and add salsa or another desired condiment. Beans, precut vegetables, and fresh fruit make a tasty, super-easy lunch. I wash, drain, and cut up fresh vegetables like broccoli and cauliflower to have for four to five lunches during the week. I store them in large ziplock bags along with a folded paper towel to absorb some of the moisture. The paper towel makes the vegetables last longer in the refrigerator."

— *Nancy Wolf*

"While fresh may be best, I was frustrated by the amount of waste. Frozen vegetable blends and minimally processed beans can be used to quickly prepare a variety of meals. By alternating among three different frozen organic vegetable blends and four different organic beans I can prepare 12 different meals the same way. First, I measure one of the frozen vegetable blends in a bowl, heat it in the microwave, add spices or condiments, and the choice of beans, heat some more, and serve. There is no waste and little to clean up. When focusing on making meals automatic, having easy meals is helpful."

— *Nathan M. Denkin*

"Always buy more than one onion, chop them all up, and put most in the freezer in ziplock bags. Then when you want chopped onion, 1 minute in the microwave thaws out the batch just enough so that you can shake out what you need for your recipe."

— *Gaye Welton*

"If you use ground meat a lot, always buy more than 1 pound at a time, brown it all at once, and freeze each pound in ziplock bags. It saves a lot of time to have it already browned and ready to go."

— *Beth Syverson*

"I keep covered bowls in the fridge for my 'extras medley,' the little extra leftover once food is weighed for a meal. I have one bowl of pieces of leftover cooked veggies, one of pieces of leftover raw veggies, and one for pieces of leftover fruit."

— *Evelyn Zoecklein*

"I love bagged slaw mix. You can add it to any meat or tofu dish and it works great with Asian spices. My favorite is broccoli slaw steamed with ground turkey and coconut aminos."

— *Sondra McNair*

"Making things like chili, with everything in one container and multiple portions, allowed me to prep my food on the weekend, and then I didn't have to worry about keeping my Bright Lines at work. Plus I could freeze some for other weeks and over time I had a nice supply of different meals all ready for me to pop out of the freezer and go!"

— *Ellen Eichen Weinman*

"At some point over the weekend I cut up zucchini squash, yellow squash, cabbage, carrots—any vegetables that are not too wet. I put them all in a big covered bowl in the fridge and each time I make a salad I just put some greens in a bowl and reach in and grab a handful of vegetables to the measure needed."

— *Michele Mariscal*

PLANNING AHEAD

To keep your Bright Lines bright and your brain humming on automaticity, here is a general rule: the more hectic your schedule is, the more you'll need to have your meals prepped in advance. Meaning, during the busiest weeks, all three meals weighed out the night before. The more relaxed and spacious your schedule is, the lighter your food prep can be and the more you can succeed by weighing and measuring a meal in the moment.

This is a lesson I learned the hard way. When I started hitting the road to give talks and attend conferences for Bright Line Eating, I found myself struggling to keep my food in order. I'd already been eating this way for 11 years, but the food prep habits I'd built at home, with a predictable schedule, weren't robust enough to carry me through the craziest days and weeks. Eventually, I learned that prepping all of my food in advance would save the day.

Let us have done the research for you. Having food prep routines that are suited to your schedule and robust enough to carry you through unforeseen emergencies and schedule changes is the linchpin to living a peaceful Bright Line life.

. . . .

"As a busy mom and career woman, I don't have time to cook during
the week. I keep a document full of my favorite meal ideas and recipes.
On Thursday, I choose my meals for the following week. On Friday,
I create my grocery list. On Saturday, I shop and prep. Then on Sunday,
I bulk cook and divide into meal portions. Through the week,
I can simply 'grab and go' the prepared items."

— *Kimberly Champion*

. . . .

"I've discovered through trial and error which proteins and veggies tend to keep me full longest. If I know that I have a long day planned, or that dinner will be later than usual, I go with the 'heavier' choices on the food list. Getting too hungry puts me in the danger zone; a little planning ahead goes a long way toward keeping my Lines bright!"

— LeeAnn Thompson

"I keep small cans of pineapple in the pantry. Drained, they are a perfect serving of fruit. If your planned fruit is over/underripe, or the kids ate it, canned pineapple is a great backup plan."

— Nikki VanDenHeuvel (Johnson)

"When I have the time, I cruise my local markets for BLE-friendly prepared foods . . . think salad bars, olive bars, prepared foods, roasted chickens. If I need just a small amount of celery, I might buy it from the salad bar! Knowing what is available, and where, is a lifesaver during busy weeks. But do be sure to read ingredient lists, even when it seems unnecessary: I discovered that the chicken in a big-box discount store has sugar in it! I never would have noticed that during my normal busy shopping sprees."

— Julie Boyd Smith

"I usually make my meals with fresh food, but sometimes I need a *fast* Bright Line meal. I've noticed other Lifers have one or two of these in their tool kit as well. My go-to is canned beans and frozen spinach. I also almost always have some jars of salsa around. I thaw the spinach in the microwave, add the correct amount of pinto or black or garbanzo beans, add some salsa as a condiment, and that plus a fruit is my lunch (or without fruit, it's my dinner). For a fat, you can dice up half an avocado on top, or just measure half an ounce of nuts. This meal tastes better than it sounds, and because the beans are canned and the spinach is frozen, I know I have the ingredients handy."

— *Julia Carol*

FEEDING YOUR FAMILY

Bright Line Eating can definitely be done whether your family is on board or not. Bright Lifers have learned how to get their own meal on the table and cook for a family without making two, three, or four separate meals to cater to everyone's tastes. For children, what I have found works well is making a Bright Line meal for everyone and then putting a big bowl of pasta or rice on the table as well from which the kids can help themselves.

The wonderful thing is that, when someone in the family starts doing Bright Line Eating, everyone benefits. Mealtimes become more regular, vegetables make a consistent showing on the table, junk food gradually vanishes. Many spouses of our Bright Lifers lose dozens of pounds without even trying. Sanity returns to mealtime, and with it, conversation, connection, and laughter.

"Most of the dinners at my house are served family style with only BLE foods. Our basic family meal plan includes 1 protein, 1 fat, 1 or 2 vegetable options, 1 fruit option, and 1 starch option. For example, last night we had pork chops with baked sweet potatoes (and butter), Southern-style green beans, and pineapple. My kids ate everything offered, while I ate the foods that work for my dinner plan, but not the starch. If I start to crave a food that I don't eat for dinner, I can always tell myself that I'll eat it for breakfast. This makes it much easier to resist foods that are 'my foods' at breakfast, but 'not my foods' at dinner. I also feel good that I'm feeding my kids mostly whole foods."

— *Heidi Stallman*

"With boys in the house, my food was getting eaten out of the fridge and cupboards before I could get home, so I've sectioned off an area in the fridge and told my boys they can eat anything unless it's in MY area. It took some time for them to understand I was serious, but now I make extra so there's a larger container for them to eat!"

— *Charlotte Coit*

> "I've learned to use frozen riced cauliflower as an ingredient in soup, which makes it taste like rice to my family. I can also mix beans and riced cauliflower with salsa to mimic beans and rice, and my family is happy to eat it!"
>
> — *Lisa Rowe*

> "I hate throwing food out, but sometimes after I measure I have something left over. I have several bags in the freezer for these bits. Banana and berries in one bag for smoothies for my kids. Veggies in another for soup or stock."
>
> — *Nikki VanDenHeuvel (Johnson)*

EATING OUTSIDE THE HOME

Eating outside the home definitely requires more planning. Over time, Bright Lifers have learned to anticipate how and when things might go awry and plan ahead so that they'll be covered. I remember the first time I learned this lesson. Early on in my journey (around 2003), I met friends for coffee midmorning, anticipating that I would be home well before lunchtime. You can guess how the day unfolded. Now I *always* bring my packed lunch. Better safe than sorry.

If you'll be eating at a restaurant, look at the menu online and make your plan when you're full from a Bright Line meal and don't have any food triggers, like the smells in the restaurant, to awaken your Saboteur. Attending a wedding or other event? Call the banquet director and explain you need a sugar- and flour-free meal with extra vegetables. Remember that you're not bothering the caterer or chef. So many people have special dietary needs these days. It's their job and they're used to it.

At social gatherings, the key is to be clear about your BLE identity. Say, "I don't eat that," rather than, "I can't eat that." And be prepared with what you're going to say if people ask questions. This can range from being 100 percent candid and open to just saying, "I'm not eating sugar or flour these days and it's helping me sleep better," or whatever feels comfortable to you.

"I will generally call ahead to a formal event and speak with the caterer to inform them of a special dietary restriction on sugar and flour. I have spent most social events looking for someone sitting alone and then conversing with them or helping out with cleanup or refilling any empty dishes or drinks. I stay away from the food table while socializing to keep from mindlessly reaching for NMF. Being of help feels better than eating and drinking NMF/NMD. Also, I've found if you walk around with a full glass or cup of something BLE-friendly, most people will not push a drink on you."

— *Kathy Hashley*

"I used to think I was confined to a restaurant's menu when eating out.
After three years of Bright Line Eating, I no longer hesitate
to ask for something that's not on the menu. If I see they have
a protein I like in another dish, I ask for it as a side order by itself.
Restaurants usually have scales in the kitchen, as they need to
weigh food for portion consistency. I often ask for a specific number
of ounces of vegetables, as a side dish if need be."

— *Julia Carol*

"I have learned that restaurant menus are created to trigger my brain,
so I look at them as little as possible. I look online before I get to the
restaurant as often as possible, and when I end up in an unexpected
restaurant I turn to the back page for sides. I can usually find some
vegetables there and order protein just the way I want (grilled, with no
butter or oil or sauce). I have even ordered a salad 'with everything on
the side' and received a bowl of lettuce surrounded with about
eight little dishes—of which I could eat two!"

— *Julie Boyd Smith*

"It is easier than most of us think to bring our own food and/or eat ahead of time. When we believe in what we are doing, other people respect it, and there won't be nearly as many critical comments or glances as we tend to fear. I realized quickly that my own embarrassment and self-doubt were the problem—*not* others' criticism. And my own self-sabotaging longing to eat off plan was and still is much more important to keep in check than anyone pushing me to eat off plan."

— *Dina Grossman*

"Soup was my workplace go-to and I wanted to figure out how to do it in a BLE-compliant way. It can be a bit of a challenge when you want to weigh and measure the individual ingredients for one person. I found a mini Crock-Pot, which is designed to allow you to bring hot foods to work. I take cut-up cooked meat I already have on hand, like chicken, plus one of the small containers of broth; weigh out and sauté onions, carrots, and other veggies in oil or butter; and put all these ingredients in the mini Crock with some spices and salsa to round out the flavors. I take it with me to the office and plug it in at my desk. That way I have a wonderful, delicious meal that takes me no time when I'm in the middle of my workday."

— *Kallie Kendle*

> "Social gatherings seem to be difficult for me, especially potlucks. I have learned to overcome this by a) being open to people asking about what I eat and sharing my journey, b) bringing a food item to contribute that is a fairly balanced meal in itself (with both protein and veggies in the recipe), and c) eating only that in appropriate portions so I am following the plan and also feeling included and satisfied."
>
> — *Chris Southwick*

> "Balsamic vinegar makes a great salad dressing! In many restaurants you can ask for some in place of or in addition to their regular dressings."
>
> — *Julie Boyd Smith*

TRAVEL

When we hit the road we put our BLE program to the test. For that reason, if at all possible, it's best not to attempt it too early in your journey. But if you have to travel, generally speaking, the more you control your own food, the better off you'll be.

Of course, there are two kinds of travel—pleasure and work. Vacationing while doing BLE might be very antithetical to your past approach to travel, when seeing something new and *tasting* something new might have been conflated in your mind. I have been traveling around the globe with Bright Lines for 16 years now and enjoyed myself thoroughly without planning my trips around "food rewards." I focus on what I will see (the ocean, the mountains, the art) and whose company I will enjoy (my children, my family, my friends)—not on what the local treat is. So first I want to reassure you that it is possible.

I cover how to take your Bright Lines on the road in depth in the Boot Camp and in my first book. In brief here I will say that there are several ways to approach it, ranging from packing every single meal for the entire trip in a big cooler if it's a road trip, to not packing anything and trusting your eyeballs in restaurants. In between are people like me, who bring their travel scale with them, even into restaurants. I also always try to stay in a home, instead of a hotel, whenever possible. It is so much easier to stay automatized if you have a kitchen. Cities where Airbnb is legal have been a godsend for me. But the linchpin is always your deep commitment to stick to your plan.

Also keep in mind to clear your schedule for one to two days when you get back for "reentry." Coming home, getting settled in, unpacking, clearing out the email inbox, doing laundry, filling up the fridge from the grocery store, doing some food prep, and getting a good night's sleep in your own time zone all require time. Give yourself the gift of NOT arriving home at 9 P.M. and having to go to work the next morning.

"I do a large commit covering every day of my trip in advance. I use it to plan my breakfasts and eat most of those with my own premeasured packets of grains, nuts, and seeds. I get a source of whole fruits, a fridge, and I pack shelf-safe almond milk in a ziplock in my checked bag. Thirty-three percent of my meals are automated and it saves me money, too. A few times I may eat out with a veggie omelet, potatoes, and fruit. Depending on where I'm staying, I may preplan lunches and dinners too, and leave myself open to changes as needed."

— *Susan Cook*

"I've found it's easy to take food on the plane. Nuts or roasted edamame for protein, and an apple for fruit. Plus cucumber for veggies or a mixture of raw veggies: carrots, cucumber, and grape tomatoes."

— *Amelia Jordan*

"All I can say about travel is plan, plan, plan.
I say it three times on purpose because I always have
plans A, B, and C! Plan A equals what, if any, food is provided
as part of the trip. Is it a conference, cruise, or resort with meals included?
If so, what are they serving? Don't be afraid to call and speak with the
catering manager. They want to accommodate you! Plan B equals what
else is available nearby? Are there restaurants or grocery stores in the
vicinity? Plan C equals bringing some food with you in case plans A and B
fall through. Bring roasted chickpeas or edamame. In my checked luggage
I bring cans of beans, a box of almond milk, seeds for fat, all preweighed
and measured. But also bring your travel food scale."

— *Kimberly Champion*

"This is a tip for driving long distance or staying somewhere unfamiliar. I always have prepackaged oatmeal, snack baggies of measured nuts and seeds, snack baggies of dry cereal and flour-free crackers, prepackaged tuna, hummus, guacamole, olives, salad dressing, and peanut butter. Then, if there's a cooler available, bagged veggies, fruit and yogurt, and hard-boiled eggs. These are all portable in a lunch bag to go on quick trips out the door or in the car. For air travel I have taken the same items in a lunch bag in my purse, minus the yogurt."

— *Kathy Hashley*

"I have purchased two plastic food containers that collapse. They were a bit expensive but are super for travel. One is just big enough to hold my breakfast or lunch. The other larger one I use for lunches or dinners. I have no trouble getting them through TSA at airports. If they do pull them out, they say, 'This looks good.' I have another plastic container for salad dressing with a snap lid. I put in only 2 ounces, which is allowed through TSA. So after eating a meal, I go into the bathroom, rinse out the containers, collapse them, and I am done. They take up very little space in my carry-on."

— *Maitreyi Margie Wilsman*

WHAT BRIGHT LIFERS SAID THEY WISH THEY'D KNOWN

In aggregate, Bright Lifers have decades of collective experience doing Bright Line Eating. And what we, as a community, have learned is that often something that seems like it's working in the short term turns out to be a poor foundation for living Happy, Thin, and Free lifelong. Here are some of the nuggets of wisdom our Bright Lifers wish they'd known when they started.

"Don't overthink breakfast."

— *Cindy Rinaman Marsch*

"To simplify food prep, premake everything, weigh out portions,
and store each serving in a separate container.
No weighing in the moment."

— *Julie Boyd Smith*

"I have found that making the shift to thinking about each meal as self-care has been a huge help. I do everything in my power to sit down at every meal without any of my old distractions—like books or TV. Then I try to arrange my food to make it appealing (not 'sexy') using the colors of my vegetables to make a beautiful plate. I also pick bags or containers and napkins that are pleasing to the eye and touch."

— *Dina Grossman*

"It took me a long time to realize that I could split my servings and have part nuts and part almond milk at breakfast."

— *Julie Boyd Smith*

"I found nuts triggering but didn't want to eliminate them because they're so healthy! To keep nuts from calling my name, I bought a Kitchen Safe, which will lock up a food for as many hours as you select. Once in the safe, they magically stop calling to me!"

— *Julia Carol*

"If, like me, you eat too fast, try eating with a baby spoon!
By eating with a baby spoon I find I slow down, enjoy my meal,
and become full. Total win! Obviously, only do this at home."

— *Mary Reisz*

"At the beginning I made a lot of measuring mistakes.
Now I always measure things in separate containers
and then combine them."

— *Lisa Rowe*

"When my weight loss slowed the first time, I adopted a set of techniques
to lighten my plan instead of cutting my portions. This has served me well
from Boot Camp through Maintenance: #1–Use almond milk for part of my
breakfast protein. #2–Reduce use of nuts and nut butters.
#3–Have more days in the week when I eat entirely plant-based
(three days minimum). #4–Eat more raw and steamed veggies
(one salad per day). #5–Eat more beans instead of meats.
#6–Eat more leafy greens instead of starchy veggies."

— *Susan Cook*

MASHA VUJANOVIC

Before

After

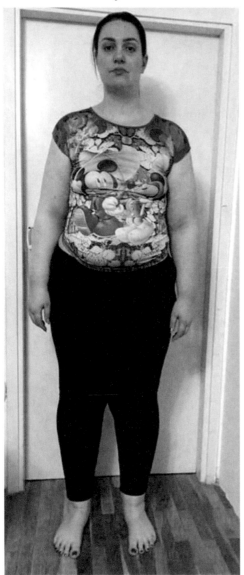

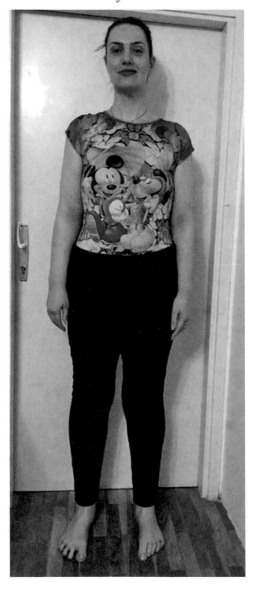

STARTING DATE **April 26, 2017**
HEAVIEST WEIGHT **343.9 pounds**
STARTING WEIGHT **302 pounds**
GOAL WEIGHT ACHIEVED **October 11, 2018**
CURRENT WEIGHT **182.9 pounds**
HEIGHT **6'2"**

I was obese for 30 years. I tried everything, but nothing gave me complete information about what to eat, what not to eat, how much to eat, how many times a day, or how to search for support—which I never had, because I didn't know I needed it.

In Serbia, where I'm from, nobody knows that obesity is an addiction problem, so there is no program like BLE. I was desperate, feeling like I lived in a jail, not able to be the "real me," and isolated from other people, because I felt so much body shame.

Since my first BLE day till now, I don't want to eat flour or sugar. Sometimes when I feel sad, fearful, or lonely, I think of food as an "emotional first aid," like it used to be. But now I know that food won't help me long term, so I don't act on it.

Now, after this miracle of coming back to a right-sized body, *everything* is easier. Problems in life come and go, but I finally feel powerful. Before now I felt pretty powerless: powerless to take back control of my weight and my body. And that feeling of powerlessness covered all the other parts of my life.

I thought I was lazy and unlovable, but the truth that I know now is that it's not my fault. I count myself very lucky to have found Bright Line Eating.

Part Three

A Year of Bright Line Meal Planning

We have created sample menu plans for a year of Bright Line Eating. Each season has a representative four-week menu plan you can repeat three times. In fact, you will notice a lot of repetition throughout the meal plans—this is intentional, both for ease of prep and use and also because as we keep saying, keeping your food repetitive and predictable will help with automaticity and resetting your Adiposity Set Point. There are seasonal menus for omnivores and whole-food plant-based eaters. Of course, please modify them as you'd like. If you have fallen in love with one of the Bright Line breakfast recipes and want to make that every day instead of what is suggested below, go for it. The same is true for lunches and dinners.

Or you may love the autumn recipes and want to eat them year-round. That is completely fine.

You also do not need to follow these suggestions at all. They are here for people who really want to take all decision-making out of this process.

As always, if something I suggest helps you feel Happy, Thin, and Free, hold on to it, nurture it, and respect it. If it throws you off in any way—more food thoughts or less peace—by all means, disregard it. Not every resource, or every recipe, will work for every person.

Omnivore's Weekly Meal Plan

WINTER
WEEK ONE

Monday	Tuesday	Wednesday	Thursday	Friday	Saturday	Sunday
BREAKFAST	**BREAKFAST**	**BREAKFAST**	**BREAKFAST**	**BREAKFAST**	**BREAKFAST**	**BREAKFAST**
4 oz. cooked oatmeal	4 oz. cooked oatmeal	4 oz. cooked oatmeal	4 oz. cooked oatmeal	4 oz. cooked oatmeal	4 oz. cooked oatmeal	4 oz. cooked oatmeal
8 oz. low-fat plain Greek yogurt	8 oz. low-fat plain Greek yogurt	8 oz. low-fat plain Greek yogurt	8 oz. low-fat plain Greek yogurt	8 oz. low-fat plain Greek yogurt	8 oz. low-fat plain Greek yogurt	8 oz. low-fat plain Greek yogurt
1 apple	1 apple	1 apple	1 apple	1 apple	1 apple	1 apple
Cinnamon	Cinnamon	Cinnamon	Cinnamon	Cinnamon	Cinnamon	Cinnamon
LUNCH	**LUNCH**	**LUNCH**	**LUNCH**	**LUNCH**	**LUNCH**	**LUNCH**
Italian Spaghetti Squash	Italian Spaghetti Squash	Italian Spaghetti Squash	Ratatouille Quick and Juicy Chicken Breasts	Chicken and Vegetable Soup	Chicken and Vegetable Soup	Mexican Zucchini Beef Skillet
1 pear	1 pear	1 pear	1 orange or 6 oz. mandarin	1 orange or 6 oz. mandarin	1 orange or 6 oz. mandarin	1 apple
			2 oz. olives	2 oz. avocado	2 oz. avocado	
DINNER	**DINNER**	**DINNER**	**DINNER**	**DINNER**	**DINNER**	**DINNER**
Basic Roasted Vegetables for All Seasons Pressure-Cooker Pulled Pork	Basic Roasted Vegetables for All Seasons Pressure-Cooker Pulled Pork	Roasted Cauliflower 4 oz. hamburger patty	Roasted Cauliflower 4 oz. hamburger patty	White Bean and Pumpkin Soup	Cauliflower Fried Rice (with eggs)	Cauliflower Fried Rice (with eggs)
8 oz. salad	8 oz. salad	8 oz. salad	8 oz. salad	4 oz. salad	¼ oz. sesame seeds	¼ oz. sesame seeds
Southwest-Style Vinaigrette	Southwest-Style Vinaigrette	Guacamole Sauce	Guacamole Sauce			

WINTER
WEEK TWO

Monday	Tuesday	Wednesday	Thursday	Friday	Saturday	Sunday
BREAKFAST	**BREAKFAST**	**BREAKFAST**	**BREAKFAST**	**BREAKFAST**	**BREAKFAST**	**BREAKFAST**
Spanish Eggs	Spanish Eggs	Spanish Eggs	Spanish Eggs	Spanish Eggs	Spanish Eggs	Spanish Eggs
LUNCH	**LUNCH**	**LUNCH**	**LUNCH**	**LUNCH**	**LUNCH**	**LUNCH**
Eggplant Parmesan	Eggplant Parmesan	Eggplant Parmesan	Grilled Salmon and Spinach Salad ½ oz. pine nuts	Grilled Salmon and Spinach Salad ½ oz. pine nuts	Mexican Zucchini Beef Skillet	Mexican Zucchini Beef Skillet
1 apple	1 apple	1 apple	1 orange	1 orange	1 pear	1 apple
DINNER	**DINNER**	**DINNER**	**DINNER**	**DINNER**	**DINNER**	**DINNER**
Lamb Stew	Lamb Stew	Hamburger and Cabbage Stir-Fry	Hamburger and Cabbage Stir-Fry	Texas Caviar	Texas Caviar	Not Your Mom's Meatloaf
1½ oz. olives	1½ oz. olives	8 oz. salad	8 oz. salad	8 oz. salad	8 oz. salad	13 oz. salad
		Southwest-Style Vinaigrette	Southwest-Style Vinaigrette			Lemon Tahini Dressing

WINTER
WEEK THREE

Monday	Tuesday	Wednesday	Thursday	Friday	Saturday	Sunday
BREAKFAST	**BREAKFAST**	**BREAKFAST**	**BREAKFAST**	**BREAKFAST**	**BREAKFAST**	**BREAKFAST**
Sweet Potato Fruit Bake	Sweet Potato Fruit Bake	Sweet Potato Fruit Bake	Sweet Potato Fruit Bake	Sweet Potato Fruit Bake	Sweet Potato Fruit Bake	Sweet Potato Fruit Bake
LUNCH	**LUNCH**	**LUNCH**	**LUNCH**	**LUNCH**	**LUNCH**	**LUNCH**
Mexican Cauliflower Rice	Mexican Cauliflower Rice	Grilled Salmon and Spinach Salad	Grilled Salmon and Spinach Salad	Italian Spaghetti Squash	Italian Spaghetti Squash	Mexican Zucchini Beef Skillet
Quick and Juicy Chicken Breasts	Quick and Juicy Chicken Breasts	2 oz. olives	2 oz. olives			
1 apple	1 apple	1 orange	1 pear	1 banana	1 apple	1 apple
DINNER	**DINNER**	**DINNER**	**DINNER**	**DINNER**	**DINNER**	**DINNER**
Not Your Mom's Meatloaf	Not Your Mom's Meatloaf	Nonie Evie's Tomato Soup	Ratatouille Quick and Juicy Chicken Breasts	Ratatouille Quick and Juicy Chicken Breasts	Hamburger and Cabbage Stir-Fry	Hamburger and Cabbage Stir-Fry
13 oz. salad	13 oz. salad		8 oz. salad	8 oz. salad	8 oz. salad	8 oz. salad
Lemon Tahini Dressing	Balsamic Vinaigrette		Southwest-Style Vinaigrette	Southwest-Style Vinaigrette	Southwest-Style Vinaigrette	Southwest-Style Vinaigrette

WINTER
WEEK FOUR

Monday	Tuesday	Wednesday	Thursday	Friday	Saturday	Sunday
BREAKFAST	**BREAKFAST**	**BREAKFAST**	**BREAKFAST**	**BREAKFAST**	**BREAKFAST**	**BREAKFAST**
Banana Rice Bake	Banana Rice Bake	Banana Rice Bake	Banana Rice Bake	Banana Rice Bake	Banana Rice Bake	Banana Rice Bake
LUNCH	**LUNCH**	**LUNCH**	**LUNCH**	**LUNCH**	**LUNCH**	**LUNCH**
Eggplant Parmesan	Eggplant Parmesan	Texas Caviar	Texas Caviar	Texas Caviar	Mexican Zucchini Beef Skillet	Mexican Zucchini Beef Skillet
1 orange or 6 oz. mandarin	1 orange or 6 oz. mandarin	1 apple	1 apple	1 orange	1 orange	1 apple
DINNER	**DINNER**	**DINNER**	**DINNER**	**DINNER**	**DINNER**	**DINNER**
Cauliflower Fried Rice (with eggs)	Cauliflower Fried Rice (with eggs)	Chicken and Vegetable Soup	Chicken and Vegetable Soup	Hamburger and Cabbage Stir-Fry	Hamburger and Cabbage Stir-Fry	Nonie Evie's Tomato Soup
¼ oz. sesame seeds	¼ oz. sesame seeds	8 oz. salad	8 oz. salad	8 oz. salad	8 oz. salad	
		Lemon Tahini Dressing	Lemon Tahini Dressing	Southwest-Style Vinaigrette	Southwest-Style Vinaigrette	

Omnivore's Weekly Meal Plan

SPRING
WEEK ONE

Monday	Tuesday	Wednesday	Thursday	Friday	Saturday	Sunday
BREAKFAST	**BREAKFAST**	**BREAKFAST**	**BREAKFAST**	**BREAKFAST**	**BREAKFAST**	**BREAKFAST**
Ricotta Oats in a Jar	Ricotta Oats in a Jar	Ricotta Oats in a Jar	Ricotta Oats in a Jar	Ricotta Oats in a Jar	Ricotta Oats in a Jar	Ricotta Oats in a Jar
LUNCH	**LUNCH**	**LUNCH**	**LUNCH**	**LUNCH**	**LUNCH**	**LUNCH**
Pressure-Cooked Beans 1 oz. cheese Pickled Beets and Cucumbers	Pressure-Cooked Beans 1 oz. cheese Pickled Beets and Cucumbers	Pressure-Cooked Beans 1 oz. cheese Pickled Beets and Cucumbers	Roasted Asparagus with Kumquats and Almonds 2 oz. sliced roast beef	Simple Tuna Salad 6 oz. salad	Simple Tuna Salad 6 oz. salad	Simple Tuna Salad 6 oz. salad
1 kiwi	1 kiwi	1 kiwi	½ oz. almonds	1 banana	1 banana	1 banana
DINNER	**DINNER**	**DINNER**	**DINNER**	**DINNER**	**DINNER**	**DINNER**
4 oz. hamburger patty Roasted Cauliflower	4 oz. hamburger patty Roasted Cauliflower	Grilled Shrimp with Arugula, Tomato, and Corn	Grilled Shrimp with Arugula, Tomato, and Corn	Grilled Shrimp with Arugula, Tomato, and Corn	Chicken Bruschetta	Fresh Corn and Black Bean Salad
8 oz. salad	8 oz. salad	6 oz. salad	6 oz. salad	6 oz. salad	4 oz. Basic Roasted Vegetables for All Seasons	8 oz. salad
Balsamic Vinaigrette	Balsamic Vinaigrette	1⅓ oz. avocado	1⅓ oz. avocado	1⅓ oz. avocado	8 oz. salad	

SPRING
WEEK TWO

Monday	Tuesday	Wednesday	Thursday	Friday	Saturday	Sunday
BREAKFAST	**BREAKFAST**	**BREAKFAST**	**BREAKFAST**	**BREAKFAST**	**BREAKFAST**	**BREAKFAST**
4 oz. cottage cheese	4 oz. cottage cheese	4 oz. cottage cheese	4 oz. cottage cheese	4 oz. cottage cheese	4 oz. cottage cheese	4 oz. cottage cheese
1 oz. Fiber One Original	1 oz. Fiber One Original	1 oz. Fiber One Original	1 oz. Fiber One Original	1 oz. Fiber One Original	1 oz. Fiber One Original	1 oz. Fiber One Original
6 oz. berries	6 oz. berries	6 oz. berries	6 oz. berries	6 oz. berries	6 oz. berries	6 oz. berries
LUNCH	**LUNCH**	**LUNCH**	**LUNCH**	**LUNCH**	**LUNCH**	**LUNCH**
Chicken and Apple Slaw	Chicken and Apple Slaw	Chicken and Apple Slaw	Curried Tuna Salad	Curried Tuna Salad	Curried Tuna Salad	3 oz. spinach leaves 2 oz. feta cheese Balsamic Vinaigrette
			6 oz. salad	6 oz. salad	6 oz. salad	3 oz. shredded carrot and zucchini
						6 oz. sliced strawberries
DINNER	**DINNER**	**DINNER**	**DINNER**	**DINNER**	**DINNER**	**DINNER**
Grilled Salmon and Spinach Salad	Grilled Salmon and Spinach Salad	6 oz. black or pinto beans	6 oz. black or pinto beans	Not Your Mom's Meatloaf	Not Your Mom's Meatloaf	Grilled Shrimp with Arugula, Tomato, and Corn
½ oz. pine nuts	½ oz. pine nuts	8 oz. salad topped with 2 oz. salsa	8 oz. salad topped with 2 oz. salsa	13 oz. salad Lemon Tahini Dressing	13 oz. salad Lemon Tahini Dressing	
8 oz. Basic Roasted Vegetables for All Seasons	8 oz. Basic Roasted Vegetables for All Seasons	Roasted Enchilada Vegetables	Roasted Enchilada Vegetables			6 oz. Zucchini noodles drizzled with ¼ oz. olive oil

Omnivore's Weekly Meal Plan

SPRING
WEEK THREE

Monday	Tuesday	Wednesday	Thursday	Friday	Saturday	Sunday
BREAKFAST	**BREAKFAST**	**BREAKFAST**	**BREAKFAST**	**BREAKFAST**	**BREAKFAST**	**BREAKFAST**
Cheese and Rice Omelet	Cheese and Rice Omelet	Cheese and Rice Omelet	Cheese and Rice Omelet	Cheese and Rice Omelet	Cheese and Rice Omelet	Cheese and Rice Omelet
6 oz. strawberries	6 oz. strawberries	6 oz. strawberries	6 oz. strawberries	6 oz. strawberries	6 oz. strawberries	6 oz. strawberries
LUNCH	**LUNCH**	**LUNCH**	**LUNCH**	**LUNCH**	**LUNCH**	**LUNCH**
Simple Egg Salad	Simple Egg Salad	Simple Egg Salad	Pressure-Cooker Pulled Pork Pickled Beets	Pressure-Cooker Pulled Pork Pickled Beets	Simple Tuna Salad	Simple Tuna Salad
6 oz. salad	6 oz. salad	6 oz. salad	½ oz. seeds	½ oz. seeds	6 oz. salad	6 oz. salad
6 oz. grapes	6 oz. grapes	6 oz. grapes	1 apple	1 apple	1 banana	1 banana
DINNER	**DINNER**	**DINNER**	**DINNER**	**DINNER**	**DINNER**	**DINNER**
Chicken Bruschetta 4 oz. zucchini noodles	Chicken Bruschetta 4 oz. zucchini noodles	Fresh Corn and Black Bean Salad	Fresh Corn and Black Bean Salad	4 oz. hamburger patty 2 oz. Fresh Salsa with Ginger Roasted asparagus	4 oz. hamburger patty 2 oz. Fresh Salsa with Ginger Roasted asparagus	Grilled Shrimp with Arugula, Tomato, and Corn
8 oz. salad	8 oz. salad	8 oz. salad	8 oz. salad	8 oz. salad	8 oz. salad	
				Balsamic Vinaigrette	Balsamic Vinaigrette	6 oz. zucchini noodles drizzled with ¼ oz. olive oil

SPRING
WEEK FOUR

Monday	Tuesday	Wednesday	Thursday	Friday	Saturday	Sunday
BREAKFAST	**BREAKFAST**	**BREAKFAST**	**BREAKFAST**	**BREAKFAST**	**BREAKFAST**	**BREAKFAST**
1 oz. Shredded Wheat 4 oz. milk 4 oz. low-fat plain Greek yogurt	1 oz. Shredded Wheat 4 oz. milk 4 oz. low-fat plain Greek yogurt	1 oz. Shredded Wheat 4 oz. milk 4 oz. low-fat plain Greek yogurt	1 oz. Shredded Wheat 4 oz. milk 4 oz. low-fat plain Greek yogurt	1 oz. Shredded Wheat 4 oz. milk 4 oz. low-fat plain Greek yogurt	1 oz. Shredded Wheat 4 oz. milk 4 oz. low-fat plain Greek yogurt	1 oz. Shredded Wheat 4 oz. milk 4 oz. low-fat plain Greek yogurt
6 oz. mixed berries	6 oz. mixed berries	6 oz. mixed berries	6 oz. mixed berries	6 oz. mixed berries	6 oz. mixed berries	6 oz. mixed berries
LUNCH	**LUNCH**	**LUNCH**	**LUNCH**	**LUNCH**	**LUNCH**	**LUNCH**
3 oz. spinach leaves 2 oz. feta cheese Balsamic Vinaigrette	3 oz. spinach leaves 2 oz. feta cheese Balsamic Vinaigrette	3 oz. spinach leaves 2 oz. feta cheese Balsamic Vinaigrette	4 oz. roast beef slices, cold Roasted Enchilada Vegetables	4 oz. roast beef slices, cold Roasted Enchilada Vegetables	4 oz. roast beef slices, cold Roasted Enchilada Vegetables	Simple Tuna Salad
3 oz. shredded carrot and zucchini	3 oz. shredded carrot and zucchini	3 oz. shredded carrot and zucchini				6 oz. salad
6 oz. sliced strawberries	6 oz. sliced strawberries	6 oz. sliced strawberries	1 apple	1 apple	1 apple	1 banana
DINNER	**DINNER**	**DINNER**	**DINNER**	**DINNER**	**DINNER**	**DINNER**
Not Your Mom's Meatloaf	Not Your Mom's Meatloaf	Quick and Juicy Chicken Breasts	Quick and Juicy Chicken Breasts	Grilled Salmon and Spinach Salad	Grilled Salmon and Spinach Salad	4 oz. Hamburger patty 2 oz. Fresh Salsa with Ginger
13 oz. salad Balsamic Vinaigrette	13 oz. salad Balsamic Vinaigrette	8 oz. salad Miso Tahini Dressing	8 oz. salad Miso Tahini Dressing	½ oz. pine nuts	½ oz. pine nuts	8 oz. salad Balsamic Vinaigrette
		6 oz. roasted asparagus	6 oz. roasted asparagus	8 oz. Basic Roasted Vegetables for All Seasons	8 oz. Basic Roasted Vegetables for All Seasons	6 oz. roasted asparagus

SUMMER
WEEK ONE

Monday	Tuesday	Wednesday	Thursday	Friday	Saturday	Sunday
BREAKFAST	**BREAKFAST**	**BREAKFAST**	**BREAKFAST**	**BREAKFAST**	**BREAKFAST**	**BREAKFAST**
Breakfast Parfait	Breakfast Parfait	Breakfast Parfait	Breakfast Parfait	Breakfast Parfait	Breakfast Parfait	Breakfast Parfait
LUNCH	**LUNCH**	**LUNCH**	**LUNCH**	**LUNCH**	**LUNCH**	**LUNCH**
Grilled Salmon and Spinach Salad	Grilled Salmon and Spinach Salad	Grilled Salmon and Spinach Salad	Quick and Juicy Chicken Breasts	Simple Tuna Salad	Simple Tuna Salad	Simple Tuna Salad
½ oz. pine nuts	½ oz. pine nuts	½ oz. pine nuts	Creole Sauce 1 oz. black olives	6 oz. salad	6 oz. salad	6 oz. salad
6 oz. berries	6 oz. berries	6 oz. berries	6 oz. melon	1 orange	1 orange	1 orange
DINNER	**DINNER**	**DINNER**	**DINNER**	**DINNER**	**DINNER**	**DINNER**
4 oz. sirloin steak Basic Roasted Vegetables for All Seasons	4 oz. sirloin steak	4 oz. sirloin steak	Caprese Salad	Quick and Juicy Chicken Breasts Basic Roasted Vegetables for All Seasons	Grilled Shrimp with Arugula, Tomato and Corn 6 oz. Spiralized zucchini drizzled with ¼ oz. olive oil	Grilled Shrimp with Arugula, Tomato and Corn 6 oz. Spiralized zucchini drizzled with ¼ oz. olive oil
8 oz. salad	Broccoli Slaw and Roasted Corn Salad	Broccoli Slaw and Roasted Corn Salad	Balsamic Vinaigrette	8 oz. salad		
Balsamic Vinaigrette				Balsamic Vinaigrette		

SUMMER
WEEK TWO

Monday	Tuesday	Wednesday	Thursday	Friday	Saturday	Sunday
BREAKFAST	**BREAKFAST**	**BREAKFAST**	**BREAKFAST**	**BREAKFAST**	**BREAKFAST**	**BREAKFAST**
4 oz. cottage cheese 1 oz. Fiber One Original 6 oz. berries	4 oz. cottage cheese 1 oz. Fiber One Original 6 oz. berries	4 oz. cottage cheese 1 oz. Fiber One Original 6 oz. berries	4 oz. cottage cheese 1 oz. Fiber One Original 6 oz. berries	4 oz. cottage cheese 1 oz. Fiber One Original 6 oz. berries	4 oz. cottage cheese 1 oz. Fiber One Original 6 oz. berries	4 oz. cottage cheese 1 oz. Fiber One Original 6 oz. berries
LUNCH	**LUNCH**	**LUNCH**	**LUNCH**	**LUNCH**	**LUNCH**	**LUNCH**
Thai Nam Sod Salad	Thai Nam Sod Salad	Thai Nam Sod Salad	Cold Stuffed Pepper 1 banana	Cold Stuffed Pepper 1 banana	Cold Stuffed Pepper 1 banana	Simple Egg Salad 6 oz. salad 6 oz. melon
DINNER	**DINNER**	**DINNER**	**DINNER**	**DINNER**	**DINNER**	**DINNER**
Chicken Bruschetta 4 oz. Basic Roasted Vegetables for All Seasons 8 oz. salad	Chicken Bruschetta 4 oz. Basic Roasted Vegetables for All Seasons 8 oz. salad	Grilled Tuna Steak with fresh squeezed lemon 14 oz. Basic Roasted Vegetables for All Seasons	Grilled Tuna Steak with fresh squeezed lemon 14 oz. Basic Roasted Vegetables for All Seasons	Basic Roasted Vegetables for All Seasons 4 oz. sirloin steak 8 oz. salad Balsamic Vinaigrette	Mediterranean Chopped Salad Basic Roasted Vegetables for All Seasons	Mediterranean Chopped Salad Basic Roasted Vegetables for All Seasons

Omnivore's Weekly Meal Plan

SUMMER
WEEK THREE

Monday	Tuesday	Wednesday	Thursday	Friday	Saturday	Sunday
BREAKFAST	**BREAKFAST**	**BREAKFAST**	**BREAKFAST**	**BREAKFAST**	**BREAKFAST**	**BREAKFAST**
1 oz. Fiber One Original 8 oz. low-fat plain Greek yogurt 6 oz. cherries	1 oz. Fiber One Original 8 oz. low-fat plain Greek yogurt 6 oz. cherries	1 oz. Fiber One Original 8 oz. low-fat plain Greek yogurt 6 oz. cherries	1 oz. Fiber One Original 8 oz. low-fat plain Greek yogurt 6 oz. cherries	1 oz. Fiber One Original 8 oz. low-fat plain Greek yogurt 6 oz. cherries	1 oz. Fiber One Original 8 oz. low-fat plain Greek yogurt 6 oz. cherries	1 oz. Fiber One Original 8 oz. low-fat plain Greek yogurt 6 oz. cherries
LUNCH	**LUNCH**	**LUNCH**	**LUNCH**	**LUNCH**	**LUNCH**	**LUNCH**
Simple Egg Salad 6 oz. salad 1 apple	Simple Egg Salad 6 oz. salad 1 apple	Simple Egg Salad 6 oz. salad 1 apple	Simple Egg Salad 6 oz. salad 1 apple	Crunchy Nut Butter Coleslaw 4 oz. hummus 6 oz. melon	Crunchy Nut Butter Coleslaw 4 oz. hummus 6 oz. melon	Simple Tuna Salad 6 oz. salad 1 orange
DINNER	**DINNER**	**DINNER**	**DINNER**	**DINNER**	**DINNER**	**DINNER**
Grilled Shrimp with Arugula, Tomato, and Corn 6 oz. grilled zucchini, drizzled with ¼ oz. olive oil	Grilled Shrimp with Arugula, Tomato, and Corn spiralized zucchini 6 oz. grilled zucchini, drizzled with ¼ oz. olive oil	Basic Roasted Vegetables for All Seasons 8 oz. salad Balsamic Vinaigrette	Quick and Juicy Chicken Breasts Basic Roasted Vegetables for All Seasons 8 oz. salad Balsamic Vinaigrette	6 oz. cooked beans Broccoli Slaw and Roasted Corn Salad	6 oz. cooked beans Broccoli Slaw and Roasted Corn Salad	Grilled Tuna Steak with fresh squeezed lemon 14 oz. Basic Roasted Vegetables for All Seasons

SUMMER
WEEK FOUR

Monday	Tuesday	Wednesday	Thursday	Friday	Saturday	Sunday
BREAKFAST	**BREAKFAST**	**BREAKFAST**	**BREAKFAST**	**BREAKFAST**	**BREAKFAST**	**BREAKFAST**
Chia Pudding	Chia Pudding	Chia Pudding	Chia Pudding	Chia Pudding	Chia Pudding	Chia Pudding
LUNCH	**LUNCH**	**LUNCH**	**LUNCH**	**LUNCH**	**LUNCH**	**LUNCH**
4 oz. sirloin steak Basic Roasted Vegetables for All Seasons ½ oz. sunflower seeds	Cold Stuffed Pepper	Cold Stuffed Pepper	Cold Stuffed Pepper	Thai Nam Sod Salad	Thai Nam Sod Salad	Thai Nam Sod Salad
6 oz. melon	1 peach or nectarine	1 peach or nectarine	1 peach or nectarine			
DINNER	**DINNER**	**DINNER**	**DINNER**	**DINNER**	**DINNER**	**DINNER**
Caprese Salad	Basic Roasted Vegetables for All Seasons 4 oz. sirloin steak	4 oz. grilled tuna steak with fresh squeezed lemon	4 oz. grilled tuna steak with fresh squeezed lemon	Mediterranean Chopped Salad	Mediterranean Chopped Salad	Chicken Bruschetta
Balsamic Vinaigrette	8 oz. salad	14 oz. Basic Roasted Vegetables for All Seasons	14 oz. Basic Roasted Vegetables for All Seasons	Basic Roasted Vegetables for All Seasons	Basic Roasted Vegetables for All Seasons	4 oz. Basic Roasted Vegetables for All Seasons
	Balsamic Vinaigrette					8 oz. salad

AUTUMN
WEEK ONE

Monday	Tuesday	Wednesday	Thursday	Friday	Saturday	Sunday
BREAKFAST	**BREAKFAST**	**BREAKFAST**	**BREAKFAST**	**BREAKFAST**	**BREAKFAST**	**BREAKFAST**
Oatmeal Rounds	Oatmeal Rounds	Oatmeal Rounds	Oatmeal Rounds	Oatmeal Rounds	Oatmeal Rounds	Oatmeal Rounds
LUNCH	**LUNCH**	**LUNCH**	**LUNCH**	**LUNCH**	**LUNCH**	**LUNCH**
Chicken and Apple Slaw	Chicken and Apple Slaw	Chicken and Apple Slaw	Pressure-Cooker Pulled Pork	Chicken and Vegetable Soup	Chicken and Vegetable Soup	Chicken and Vegetable Soup
			Charred Green Beans	1 pear	1 pear	1 pear
			1 orange	2 oz. avocado	2 oz. avocado	2 oz. avocado
DINNER	**DINNER**	**DINNER**	**DINNER**	**DINNER**	**DINNER**	**DINNER**
Caprese Salad	Caprese Salad	Pressure-Cooker Pulled Pork Charred Green Beans	Pressure-Cooker Pulled Pork Charred Green Beans	Grilled Shrimp with Arugula, Tomato, and Corn	Grilled Shrimp with Arugula, Tomato, and Corn	Very Veggie Chili
Balsamic Vinaigrette	Balsamic Vinaigrette	8 oz. salad	8 oz. salad	6 oz. salad	6 oz. salad	
				⅔ serving Hummus Dressing	⅔ serving Hummus Dressing	

AUTUMN
WEEK TWO

Monday	Tuesday	Wednesday	Thursday	Friday	Saturday	Sunday
BREAKFAST	**BREAKFAST**	**BREAKFAST**	**BREAKFAST**	**BREAKFAST**	**BREAKFAST**	**BREAKFAST**
Banana Rice Bake	Banana Rice Bake	Banana Rice Bake	Banana Rice Bake	Banana Rice Bake	Banana Rice Bake	Banana Rice Bake
LUNCH	**LUNCH**	**LUNCH**	**LUNCH**	**LUNCH**	**LUNCH**	**LUNCH**
Curried Tuna Salad	Curried Tuna Salad	Curried Tuna Salad	4 oz. hamburger patty Basic Roasted Vegetables for All Seasons 1 pear	4 oz. hamburger patty Basic Roasted Vegetables for All Seasons 1 pear	4 oz. hamburger patty Basic Roasted Vegetables for All Seasons 1 pear	Eggplant Parmesan 6 oz. berries
6 oz. salad	6 oz. salad	6 oz. salad	Guacamole Sauce	Guacamole Sauce	Guacamole Sauce	
DINNER	**DINNER**	**DINNER**	**DINNER**	**DINNER**	**DINNER**	**DINNER**
Mexican Zucchini Beef Skillet	Mexican Zucchini Beef Skillet	Mexican Zucchini Beef Skillet	Very Veggie Chili	Italian Spaghetti Squash (with chicken)	Italian Spaghetti Squash (with chicken)	Quick and Juicy Chicken Breasts 6 oz. roasted root vegetables
8 oz. salad	8 oz. salad			8 oz. salad	8 oz. salad	8 oz. salad Miso Tahini Dressing

AUTUMN
WEEK THREE

Monday	Tuesday	Wednesday	Thursday	Friday	Saturday	Sunday
BREAKFAST	**BREAKFAST**	**BREAKFAST**	**BREAKFAST**	**BREAKFAST**	**BREAKFAST**	**BREAKFAST**
Spanish Eggs	Spanish Eggs	Spanish Eggs	Spanish Eggs	Spanish Eggs	Spanish Eggs	Spanish Egg
LUNCH	**LUNCH**	**LUNCH**	**LUNCH**	**LUNCH**	**LUNCH**	**LUNCH**
4 oz. hamburger patty 6 oz. salad	Chicken and Vegetable Soup	Chicken and Vegetable Soup	Chicken and Vegetable Soup	Mexican Zucchini Beef Skillet	Mexican Zucchini Beef Skillet	Mexican Zucchini Beef Skillet
1 banana	1 pear	1 pear	1 pear	6 oz. berries	6 oz. berries	6 oz. berries
Southwest Style Vinaigrette	2 oz. avocado	2 oz. avocado	2 oz. avocado			
DINNER	**DINNER**	**DINNER**	**DINNER**	**DINNER**	**DINNER**	**DINNER**
Very Veggie Chili	Grilled Shrimp with Arugula, Tomato, and Corn	Grilled Shrimp with Arugula, Tomato, and Corn	Pressure-Cooker Pulled Pork Charred Green Beans	Pressure-Cooker Pulled Pork Charred Green Beans	Chicken Fajita Bowl	Chicken Fajita Bowl
	6 oz. salad	6 oz. salad				
	⅔ serving Hummus Dressing	⅔ serving Hummus Dressing	8 oz. salad	8 oz. salad		

AUTUMN
WEEK FOUR

Monday	Tuesday	Wednesday	Thursday	Friday	Saturday	Sunday
BREAKFAST	**BREAKFAST**	**BREAKFAST**	**BREAKFAST**	**BREAKFAST**	**BREAKFAST**	**BREAKFAST**
4 oz. cottage cheese 1 oz. Shredded Wheat 6 oz. blueberries	4 oz. cottage cheese 1 oz. Shredded Wheat 6 oz. blueberries	4 oz. cottage cheese 1 oz. Shredded Wheat 6 oz. blueberries	4 oz. cottage cheese 1 oz. Shredded Wheat 6 oz. blueberries	4 oz. cottage cheese 1 oz. Shredded Wheat 6 oz. blueberries	4 oz. cottage cheese 1 oz. Shredded Wheat 6 oz. blueberries	4 oz. cottage cheese 1 oz. Shredded Wheat 6 oz. blueberries
LUNCH	**LUNCH**	**LUNCH**	**LUNCH**	**LUNCH**	**LUNCH**	**LUNCH**
Chicken and Apple Slaw	Chicken and Apple Slaw	Mexican Zucchini Beef Skillet 6 oz. berries	Mexican Zucchini Beef Skillet 6 oz. berries	Curried Tuna Salad 6 oz. salad	Curried Tuna Salad 6 oz. salad	Curried Tuna Salad 6 oz. salad
DINNER	**DINNER**	**DINNER**	**DINNER**	**DINNER**	**DINNER**	**DINNER**
Very Veggie Chili	Cauliflower Fried Rice ¼ oz. sesame oil	Cauliflower Fried Rice ¼ oz. sesame oil	Cauliflower Fried Rice 1/4 oz. sesame oil	Italian Spaghetti Squash (with chicken) 8 oz. salad	Italian Spaghetti Squash (with chicken) 8 oz. salad	Nonie Evie's Tomato Soup

IRINA LEE

Before

After

STARTING DATE October 8, 2015
STARTING WEIGHT 178 pounds
GOAL WEIGHT ACHIEVED April 24, 2016
CURRENT WEIGHT 140 pounds
HEIGHT 5'7⅓"

I come from a family of renowned Norwegian chefs. In my early childhood, my father worked as a manager for a chain of bakeries and restaurants. As a result, there was always lots of food around and I developed a deep and loving relationship with sugar and flour at an early age.

When I was eight, my mother passed away of cancer. Shortly after, I learned to cook. I had two sets of recipes. First, the healthy ones that I would cook for my family. Then the other "recipes," the stuff I would whip together when no one was watching—the combinations of sugar and flour that I would stir together without any intention of baking anything.

Those sugar-and-flour cocktails were my drug of choice for years. Or, to be honest, decades.

I could stay "sober" for months. Sometimes thinking, *Hey! Maybe I no longer need those old strategies to cope* . . . But I was wrong. At some point, I would always turn back to my old habits, despite the fact that I KNEW it would give me stomach pains, digestion trouble, and an unbearable burden of shame and self-hate.

This lasted until October 2015, the moment when I found Bright Line Eating and signed up for the Boot Camp. I was five months shy of my 40th birthday and had struggled with my weight and feelings of hopelessness for more than 30 years. I was tired. I was exhausted. And I was willing to surrender.

Today, when it comes to my food, I no longer search the Internet for advanced recipes or a ton of ingredients to spice up my meals. On the contrary, I love to "KISS": Keep It Super Simple.

I promise you, it's doable. And so worth it. I was stuck in a prison of recurring food thoughts and cravings for too many years. Living life on the Bright Side has provided a freedom I didn't even know existed.

Today, I enjoy my life. I enjoy my food. I enjoy my own company, and I enjoy the company of others, especially my kids. They now have a mother who is happy with herself, and who has enough energy and patience to be the mother they deserve to have.

Whole-Food
Plant-Based
Weekly
Meal Plan

WINTER
WEEK ONE

Monday	Tuesday	Wednesday	Thursday	Friday	Saturday	Sunday
BREAKFAST	**BREAKFAST**	**BREAKFAST**	**BREAKFAST**	**BREAKFAST**	**BREAKFAST**	**BREAKFAST**
4 oz. cooked oatmeal 6 oz. plant-based yogurt ½ oz. ground flax 6 oz. grapefruit	4 oz. cooked oatmeal 6 oz. plant-based yogurt ½ oz. ground flax 6 oz. grapefruit	4 oz. cooked oatmeal 6 oz. plant-based yogurt ½ oz. ground flax 6 oz. grapefruit	4 oz. cooked oatmeal 6 oz. plant-based yogurt ½ oz. ground flax 6 oz. grapefruit	4 oz. cooked oatmeal 6 oz. plant-based yogurt ½ oz. ground flax 6 oz. grapefruitt	4 oz. cooked oatmeal 6 oz. plant-based yogurt ½ oz. ground flax 6 oz. grapefruit	4 oz. cooked oatmeal 6 oz. plant-based yogurt ½ oz. ground flax 6 oz. grapefruit
LUNCH	**LUNCH**	**LUNCH**	**LUNCH**	**LUNCH**	**LUNCH**	**LUNCH**
6 oz. roasted butternut squash 6 oz. cooked beans ½ oz. pine nuts	6 oz. roasted butternut squash 6 oz. cooked beans ½ oz. pine nuts	6 oz. roasted butternut squash 6 oz. cooked beans ½ oz. pine nuts	Quinoa and Chickpea Salad	Quinoa and Chickpea Salad	Quinoa and Chickpea Salad	Chipotle Vegan Sausage and White Bean Stew 2 oz. avocado
1 pear	1 pear	1 pear	1 orange or 6 oz. mandarin	1 orange or 6 oz. mandarin	1 orange or 6 oz. mandarin	1 apple
DINNER	**DINNER**	**DINNER**	**DINNER**	**DINNER**	**DINNER**	**DINNER**
Cauliflower Fried Rice (with tofu)	Cauliflower Fried Rice (with tofu)	Very Veggie Chili	Very Veggie Chili	Latin Stuffed Peppers	Latin Stuffed Peppers	Coconut Curry Stir Fry
¼ oz. sliced almonds	¼ oz. sliced almonds					

WINTER
WEEK TWO

Monday	Tuesday	Wednesday	Thursday	Friday	Saturday	Sunday
BREAKFAST	**BREAKFAST**	**BREAKFAST**	**BREAKFAST**	**BREAKFAST**	**BREAKFAST**	**BREAKFAST**
All About Oats	All About Oats	All About Oats	All About Oats	All About Oats	All About Oats	All About Oats
LUNCH	**LUNCH**	**LUNCH**	**LUNCH**	**LUNCH**	**LUNCH**	**LUNCH**
4 oz. veggie burger 6 oz. salad Guacamole Sauce	4 oz. veggie burger 6 oz. salad Guacamole Sauce	4 oz. veggie burger 6 oz. salad Guacamole Sauce	Steamed Kale and Lentil Bowl	Steamed Kale and Lentil Bowl	Susan's Tasty Tofu or Tempeh Roasted Cauliflower Miso Tahini Dressing	Susan's Tasty Tofu or Tempeh Roasted Cauliflower Miso Tahini Dressing
6 oz. sliced apple	6 oz. sliced apple	6 oz. sliced apple			6 oz. pineapple	6 oz. pineapple
DINNER	**DINNER**	**DINNER**	**DINNER**	**DINNER**	**DINNER**	**DINNER**
Very Veggie Chili	Very Veggie Chili	6 oz. black beans Basic Roasted Vegetables for All Seasons 2 oz. salsa	6 oz. black beans Basic Roasted Vegetables for All Seasons 2 oz. salsa	Texas Caviar	Texas Caviar	"Cream" of Broccoli soup (with tofu)
		8 oz. salad Southwest-Style Vinaigrette	8 oz. salad Southwest-Style Vinaigrette	8 oz. salad	8 oz. salad	

Whole-Food Plant-Based Weekly Meal Plan

WINTER
WEEK THREE

Monday	Tuesday	Wednesday	Thursday	Friday	Saturday	Sunday
BREAKFAST	**BREAKFAST**	**BREAKFAST**	**BREAKFAST**	**BREAKFAST**	**BREAKFAST**	**BREAKFAST**
Beans, Sweet Potatoes, and Apples, Oh My!	Beans, Sweet Potatoes, and Apples, Oh My!	Beans, Sweet Potatoes, and Apples, Oh My!	Beans, Sweet Potatoes, and Apples, Oh My!	Beans, Sweet Potatoes, and Apples, Oh My!	Beans, Sweet Potatoes, and Apples, Oh My!	Beans, Sweet Potatoes, and Apples, Oh My!
LUNCH	**LUNCH**	**LUNCH**	**LUNCH**	**LUNCH**	**LUNCH**	**LUNCH**
4 oz. hummus 6 oz. carrots Southwest Style Vinaigrette	4 oz. hummus 6 oz. carrots Southwest Style Vinaigrette	4 oz. vegan sausage 6 oz. salad Southwest Style Vinaigrette	Susan's Tasty Tofu or Tempeh Basic Roasted Vegetables for All Seasons Miso Tahini Vinaigrette	Susan's Tasty Tofu or Tempeh Basic Roasted Vegetables for All Seasons Miso Tahini Vinaigrette	Susan's Tasty Tofu or Tempeh Basic Roasted Vegetables for All Seasons Miso Tahini Vinaigrette	Susan's Tasty Tofu or Tempeh Basic Roasted Vegetables for All Seasons Miso Tahini Vinaigrette
6 oz. mango	6 oz. mango	6 oz. mango	6 oz. sliced apple	6 oz. sliced apple	1 pear	1 pear
DINNER	**DINNER**	**DINNER**	**DINNER**	**DINNER**	**DINNER**	**DINNER**
Latin Stuffed Peppers	Latin Stuffed Peppers	Cauliflower Fried Rice (with tofu)	Cauliflower Fried Rice (with tofu)	Cauliflower Fried Rice (with tofu)	Eggplant Parmesan with tofu and nondairy cheese	Eggplant Parmesan with tofu and nondairy cheese
		¼ oz. sliced almonds	¼ oz. sliced almonds	¼ oz. sliced almonds	8 oz. roasted broccoli	8 oz. roasted broccoli

WINTER
WEEK FOUR

Monday	Tuesday	Wednesday	Thursday	Friday	Saturday	Sunday
BREAKFAST	**BREAKFAST**	**BREAKFAST**	**BREAKFAST**	**BREAKFAST**	**BREAKFAST**	**BREAKFAST**
6 oz. beans 4 oz. cooked oatmeal 1 apple	6 oz. beans 4 oz. cooked oatmeal 1 apple	6 oz. beans 4 oz. cooked oatmeal 1 apple	6 oz. beans 4 oz. cooked oatmeal 1 apple	6 oz. beans 4 oz. cooked oatmeal 1 apple	6 oz. beans 4 oz. cooked oatmeal 1 apple	6 oz. beans 4 oz. cooked oatmeal 1 apple
LUNCH	**LUNCH**	**LUNCH**	**LUNCH**	**LUNCH**	**LUNCH**	**LUNCH**
6 oz. cooked white beans 6 oz. salad	6 oz. cooked white beans 6 oz. salad	Texas Caviar	Texas Caviar	Peppers and Tomato Sauce over 4 oz. scrambled tofu Slow-Cooker Southern-Style Green Beans	Peppers and Tomato Sauce over 4 oz. scrambled tofu Slow-Cooker Southern-Style Green Beans	Garlic Roasted Beets 6 oz. pinto beans
1 orange or 6 oz. mandarin	1 orange or 6 oz. mandarin	1 apple	1 apple	½ oz. pumpkin seeds	½ oz. pumpkin seeds	½ oz. sunflower seeds
Miso Tahini Dressing	Miso Tahini Dressing			6 oz. papaya	6 oz. papaya	6 oz. papaya
DINNER	**DINNER**	**DINNER**	**DINNER**	**DINNER**	**DINNER**	**DINNER**
Cauliflower Fried Rice (with tofu)	Cauliflower Fried Rice (with tofu)	6 oz. white beans Creole Sauce over 8 oz. roasted Brussels sprouts	6 oz. white beans Creole Sauce over 8 oz. roasted Brussels sprouts	Susan's Tasty Tofu or Tempeh Cinnamon Winter Squash	Susan's Tasty Tofu or Tempeh Cinnamon Winter Squash	"Cream" of Broccoli Soup (with tofu)
¼ oz. sliced almonds	¼ oz. sliced almonds	¼ oz. oil	¼ oz. oil	8 oz. salad	8 oz. salad	
				Lemon Tahini Dressing	Lemon Tahini Dressing	

Whole-Food Plant-Based Weekly Meal Plan

SPRING
WEEK ONE

Monday	Tuesday	Wednesday	Thursday	Friday	Saturday	Sunday
BREAKFAST	**BREAKFAST**	**BREAKFAST**	**BREAKFAST**	**BREAKFAST**	**BREAKFAST**	**BREAKFAST**
All About Oats	All About Oats	All About Oats	All About Oats	All About Oats	All About Oats	All About Oats
LUNCH	**LUNCH**	**LUNCH**	**LUNCH**	**LUNCH**	**LUNCH**	**LUNCH**
Garlic Roasted Beets 6 oz. pinto beans ½ oz. seeds	Garlic Roasted Beets 6 oz. pinto beans ½ oz. seeds	Garlic Roasted Beets 6 oz. pinto beans ½ oz. seeds	Quinoa and Chickpea Salad	Quinoa and Chickpea Salad	Quinoa and Chickpea Salad	Moroccan Carrot Bowl
1 apple	1 apple	1 apple	1 pear	1 pear	1 pear	1 apple
DINNER	**DINNER**	**DINNER**	**DINNER**	**DINNER**	**DINNER**	**DINNER**
Moroccan Carrot Bowl	Moroccan Carrot Bowl	Crunchy Nut Butter Coleslaw	Crunchy Nut Butter Coleslaw	Susan's Tasty Tofu or Tempeh	Susan's Tasty Tofu or Tempeh	6 oz. lentils
8 oz. grilled zucchini	8 oz. grilled zucchini	4 oz. shelled edamame	4 oz. shelled edamame	14 oz. lettuce, red peppers, radishes, cherry tomatoes, and carrots	14 oz. lettuce, red peppers, radishes, cherry tomatoes, and carrots	6 oz. grilled asparagus
		8 oz. roasted broccoli	8 oz. roasted broccoli	Hummus Dressing	Hummus Dressing	Lemon Tahini Dressing
						8 oz. salad

SPRING
WEEK TWO

Monday	Tuesday	Wednesday	Thursday	Friday	Saturday	Sunday
BREAKFAST	**BREAKFAST**	**BREAKFAST**	**BREAKFAST**	**BREAKFAST**	**BREAKFAST**	**BREAKFAST**
6 oz. plant-based yogurt 4 oz. sweet potato ½ oz. ground flax 6 oz. berries	6 oz. plant-based yogurt 4 oz. sweet potato ½ oz. ground flax 6 oz. berries	6 oz. plant-based yogurt 4 oz. sweet potato ½ oz. ground flax 6 oz. berries	6 oz. plant-based yogurt 4 oz. sweet potato ½ oz. ground flax 6 oz. berries	6 oz. plant-based yogurt 4 oz. sweet potato ½ oz. ground flax 6 oz. berries	6 oz. plant-based yogurt 4 oz. sweet potato ½ oz. ground flax 6 oz. berries	6 oz. plant-based yogurt 4 oz. sweet potato ½ oz. ground flax 6 oz. berries
LUNCH	**LUNCH**	**LUNCH**	**LUNCH**	**LUNCH**	**LUNCH**	**LUNCH**
Pickled Beets and Cucumbers 4 oz. hummus	Pickled Beets and Cucumbers 4 oz. hummus	Pickled Beets and Cucumbers 4 oz. hummus	Pickled Beets and Cucumbers 4 oz. hummus	Moroccan Carrot Bowl	Moroccan Carrot Bowl	4 oz. plant-based yogurt Crunchy Nut Butter Slaw
½ oz. pecans	½ oz. pecans	½ oz. pecans	½ oz. pecans			1 oz. nuts
1 peach or nectarine	1 peach or nectarine	1 peach or nectarine	1 peach or nectarine	1 orange	1 orange	1 orange
DINNER	**DINNER**	**DINNER**	**DINNER**	**DINNER**	**DINNER**	**DINNER**
Moroccan Carrot Bowl	Fresh Corn and Black Bean Salad	Fresh Corn and Black Bean Salad	Mediterranean Chopped Salad	Mediterranean Chopped Salad	"Cream" of Broccoli Soup (with tofu)	"Cream" of Broccoli Soup (with tofu)
8 oz. roasted asparagus	8 oz. roasted leeks and mushrooms	8 oz. roasted leeks and mushrooms	6 oz. cooked baby squash	6 oz. cooked baby squash		

Whole-Food Plant-Based Weekly Meal Plan

SPRING
WEEK THREE

Monday	Tuesday	Wednesday	Thursday	Friday	Saturday	Sunday
BREAKFAST	**BREAKFAST**	**BREAKFAST**	**BREAKFAST**	**BREAKFAST**	**BREAKFAST**	**BREAKFAST**
6 oz. beans 4 oz. cooked oatmeal 6 oz. raspberries	6 oz. beans 4 oz. cooked oatmeal 6 oz. raspberries	6 oz. beans 4 oz. cooked oatmeal 6 oz. raspberries	6 oz. beans 4 oz. cooked oatmeal 6 oz. raspberries	6 oz. beans 4 oz. cooked oatmeal 6 oz. raspberries	6 oz. beans 4 oz. cooked oatmeal 6 oz. raspberries	6 oz. beans 4 oz. cooked oatmeal 6 oz. raspberries
LUNCH	**LUNCH**	**LUNCH**	**LUNCH**	**LUNCH**	**LUNCH**	**LUNCH**
6 oz. black beans 6 oz. salad topped with 1 tbsp chili powder, 2 tbsp salsa and 2 oz. diced avocado	6 oz. black beans 6 oz. salad topped with 1 tbsp chili powder, 2 tbsp salsa and 2 oz. diced avocado	4 oz. plant-based yogurt Crunchy Nut Butter Coleslaw 1 oz. nuts	4 oz. plant-based yogurt Crunchy Nut Butter Coleslaw 1 oz. nuts	6 oz. black beans, Basic Roasted Vegetables for All Seasons (cold) Balsamic Vinaigrette	6 oz. black beans, Basic Roasted Vegetables for All Seasons (cold) Balsamic Vinaigrette	4 oz. plant-based yogurt Crunchy Nut Butter Coleslaw 1 oz. nuts
1 orange	1 orange	1 apple	1 apple	6 oz. strawberries	6 oz. strawberries	1 orange
DINNER	**DINNER**	**DINNER**	**DINNER**	**DINNER**	**DINNER**	**DINNER**
Crunchy Nut Butter Coleslaw	Crunchy Nut Butter Coleslaw	Moroccan Carrot Bowl	Mediterranean Chopped Salad	Mediterranean Chopped Salad	Fresh Corn and Black Bean Salad	Fresh Corn and Black Bean Salad
4 oz. shelled edamame	4 oz. shelled edamame	8 oz. salad	Pickled Beets	Pickled Beets	8 oz. salad	8 oz. salad
8 oz. grilled zucchini	8 oz. grilled zucchini					

SPRING
WEEK FOUR

Monday	Tuesday	Wednesday	Thursday	Friday	Saturday	Sunday
BREAKFAST	**BREAKFAST**	**BREAKFAST**	**BREAKFAST**	**BREAKFAST**	**BREAKFAST**	**BREAKFAST**
4 oz. cooked oatmeal 6 oz. plant-based yogurt ½ oz. ground flax 1 orange	4 oz. cooked oatmeal 6 oz. plant-based yogurt ½ oz. ground flax 1 orange	4 oz. cooked oatmeal 6 oz. plant-based yogurt ½ oz. ground flax 1 orange	4 oz. cooked oatmeal 6 oz. plant-based yogurt ½ oz. ground flax 1 orange	4 oz. cooked oatmeal 6 oz. plant-based yogurt ½ oz. ground flax 1 orange	4 oz. cooked oatmeal 6 oz. plant-based yogurt ½ oz. ground flax 1 orange	4 oz. cooked oatmeal 6 oz. plant-based yogurt ½ oz. ground flax 1 orange
LUNCH	**LUNCH**	**LUNCH**	**LUNCH**	**LUNCH**	**LUNCH**	**LUNCH**
Susan's Tasty Tofu or Tempeh 6 oz. salad Miso Tahini Dressing	Susan's Tasty Tofu or Tempeh 6 oz. salad Miso Tahini Dressing	Susan's Tasty Tofu or Tempeh 6 oz. salad Miso Tahini Dressing	Pickled Beets and Cucumbers 4 oz. hummus ½ oz. pecans	Pickled Beets and Cucumbers 4 oz. hummus ½ oz. pecans	Pickled Beets and Cucumbers 4 oz. hummus ½ oz. pecans	Moroccan Carrot Bowl
1 apple	1 apple	1 apple	1 peach or nectarine	1 peach or nectarine	1 peach or nectarine	1 pear
DINNER	**DINNER**	**DINNER**	**DINNER**	**DINNER**	**DINNER**	**DINNER**
Broccoli Slaw and Roasted Corn Salad	Broccoli Slaw and Roasted Corn Salad	Broccoli Slaw and Roasted Corn Salad	6 oz. cooked lentils Sun-Dried Tomato and Kale Salad Basic Roasted Vegetables for All Seasons	6 oz. cooked lentils Sun-Dried Tomato and Kale Salad Basic Roasted Vegetables for All Seasons	6 oz. cooked lentils Sun-Dried Tomato and Kale Salad Basic Roasted Vegetables for All Seasons	6 oz. black beans 8 oz. salad topped with 1 tbsp chili powder, 2 tbsp salsa and 2 oz. diced avocado
6 oz. cooked beans	6 oz. cooked beans	6 oz. cooked beans	1⅓ oz. of guacamole	1⅓ oz. of guacamole	1⅓ oz. of guacamole	Basic Roasted Vegetables for All Seasons

Whole-Food Plant-Based Weekly Meal Plan

SUMMER
WEEK ONE

Monday	Tuesday	Wednesday	Thursday	Friday	Saturday	Sunday
BREAKFAST	**BREAKFAST**	**BREAKFAST**	**BREAKFAST**	**BREAKFAST**	**BREAKFAST**	**BREAKFAST**
All About Oats	All About Oats	All About Oats	All About Oats	All About Oats	All About Oats	All About Oats
LUNCH	**LUNCH**	**LUNCH**	**LUNCH**	**LUNCH**	**LUNCH**	**LUNCH**
Cold Stuffed Pepper	Cold Stuffed Pepper	Cold Stuffed Pepper	Roasted Asparagus with Kumquats and Almonds	Pickled Beets and Cucumbers 4 oz. hummus topped with ½ oz. hazelnuts	Pickled Beets and Cucumbers 4 oz. hummus topped with ½ oz. hazelnuts	Pickled Beets and Cucumbers 4 oz. hummus topped with ½ oz. hazelnuts
6 oz. strawberries	6 oz. strawberries	6 oz. strawberries	4 oz. hummus	6 oz. melon	6 oz. melon	6 oz. melon
DINNER	**DINNER**	**DINNER**	**DINNER**	**DINNER**	**DINNER**	**DINNER**
Moroccan Carrot Bowl	Moroccan Carrot Bowl	Fresh Corn and Black Bean Salad	Fresh Corn and Black Bean Salad	8 oz. Mixed green salad with 1 tbsp chili powder, 6 oz. pinto beans, 2 oz. avocado, and 2 tbsp. balsamic vinegar	8 oz. Mixed green salad with 1 tbsp chili powder, 6 oz. pinto beans, 2 oz. avocado, and 2 tbsp. balsamic vinegar	Susan's Tasty Tofu or Tempeh 14 oz. Spiralized yellow squash
8 oz. raw vegetables	8 oz. raw vegetables	8 oz. Basic Roasted Vegetables for All Seasons	8 oz. Basic Roasted Vegetables for All Seasons	Basic Roasted Vegetables for All Seasons	Basic Roasted Vegetables for All Seasons	Miso Tahini Vinaigrette

SUMMER
WEEK TWO

Monday	Tuesday	Wednesday	Thursday	Friday	Saturday	Sunday
BREAKFAST	**BREAKFAST**	**BREAKFAST**	**BREAKFAST**	**BREAKFAST**	**BREAKFAST**	**BREAKFAST**
4 oz. cooked oatmeal 4 oz. plant-based yogurt 1 oz. hemp hearts 6 oz. blueberries	4 oz. cooked oatmeal 4 oz. plant-based yogurt 1 oz. hemp hearts 6 oz. blueberries	4 oz. cooked oatmeal 4 oz. plant-based yogurt 1 oz. hemp hearts 6 oz. blueberries	4 oz. cooked oatmeal 4 oz. plant-based yogurt 1 oz. hemp hearts 6 oz. blueberries	4 oz. cooked oatmeal 4 oz. plant-based yogurt 1 oz. hemp hearts 6 oz. blueberries	4 oz. cooked oatmeal 4 oz. plant-based yogurt 1 oz. hemp hearts 6 oz. blueberries	4 oz. cooked oatmeal 4 oz. plant-based yogurt 1 oz. hemp hearts 6 oz. blueberries
LUNCH	**LUNCH**	**LUNCH**	**LUNCH**	**LUNCH**	**LUNCH**	**LUNCH**
Moroccan Carrot Bowl	Moroccan Carrot Bowl	Moroccan Carrot Bowl	Moroccan Carrot Bowl	Fresh Corn and Black Bean Salad	Fresh Corn and Black Bean Salad	Fresh Corn and Black Bean Salad
1 apple	1 apple	6 oz. blueberries	6 oz. blueberries	6 oz. blueberries	1 peach or nectarine	1 peach or nectarine
DINNER	**DINNER**	**DINNER**	**DINNER**	**DINNER**	**DINNER**	**DINNER**
6 oz. garbanzo beans 14 oz. spinach greens, cherry tomatoes, red onions Southwest-Style Vinaigrette	6 oz. garbanzo beans 14 oz. spinach greens, cherry tomatoes, red onions Southwest-Style Vinaigrette	6 oz. garbanzo beans 14 oz. spinach greens, cherry tomatoes, red onions Southwest-Style Vinaigrette	Mexican Cauliflower Rice 6 oz. black beans 8 oz. grilled peppers	Susan's Tasty Tofu or Tempeh 14 oz. Spiralized yellow squash Miso Tahini Vinaigrette	Susan's Tasty Tofu or Tempeh 14 oz. Spiralized yellow squash Miso Tahini Vinaigrette	Susan's Tasty Tofu or Tempeh Roasted Enchilada Vegetables 8 oz. salad topped with 2 oz. salsa

Whole-Food Plant-Based Weekly Meal Plan

SUMMER

WEEK THREE

Monday	Tuesday	Wednesday	Thursday	Friday	Saturday	Sunday
BREAKFAST	**BREAKFAST**	**BREAKFAST**	**BREAKFAST**	**BREAKFAST**	**BREAKFAST**	**BREAKFAST**
4 oz. cooked rice 4 oz. unsweetened soy milk 1 oz. hemp hearts 6 oz. mixed berries	4 oz. cooked rice 4 oz. unsweetened soy milk 1 oz. hemp hearts 6 oz. mixed berries	4 oz. cooked rice 4 oz. unsweetened soy milk 1 oz. hemp hearts 6 oz. mixed berries	4 oz. cooked rice 4 oz. unsweetened soy milk 1 oz. hemp hearts 6 oz. mixed berries	4 oz. cooked rice 4 oz. unsweetened soy milk 1 oz. hemp hearts 6 oz. mixed berries	4 oz. cooked rice 4 oz. unsweetened soy milk 1 oz. hemp hearts 6 oz. mixed berries	4 oz. cooked rice 4 oz. unsweetened soy milk 1 oz. hemp hearts 6 oz. mixed berries
LUNCH	**LUNCH**	**LUNCH**	**LUNCH**	**LUNCH**	**LUNCH**	**LUNCH**
Fresh Corn and Black Bean Salad	Fresh Corn and Black Bean Salad	6 oz. garbanzo beans 6 oz. spinach greens, cherry tomatoes, red onions Southwest-Style Vinaigrette	6 oz. garbanzo beans 6 oz. spinach greens, cherry tomatoes, red onions Southwest-Style Vinaigrette	6 oz. garbanzo beans 6 oz. spinach greens, cherry tomatoes, red onions Southwest-Style Vinaigrette	6 oz. garbanzo beans 6 oz. spinach greens, cherry tomatoes, red onions Southwest-Style Vinaigrette	Pickled Beets and Cucumbers 6 oz. beans ½ oz. hazelnuts
1 peach or nectarine	1 peach or nectarine	6 oz. melon	1 apple	1 apple	1 apple	6 oz. melon
DINNER	**DINNER**	**DINNER**	**DINNER**	**DINNER**	**DINNER**	**DINNER**
Susan's Tasty Tofu or Tempeh 14 oz. Spiralized yellow squash Miso Tahini Vinaigrette	Crunchy Nut Butter Coleslaw 4 oz. tofu	Crunchy Nut Butter Coleslaw 4 oz. tofu	Mexican Cauliflower Rice 6 oz. black beans	Mexican Cauliflower Rice 6 oz. black beans	Fresh Corn and Black Bean Salad	Fresh Corn and Black Bean Salad
	8 oz. roasted Brussels sprouts	8 oz. roasted Brussels sprouts	8 oz. roasted asparagus	8 oz. roasted asparagus	8 oz. grilled zucchini	8 oz. grilled zucchini

SUMMER
WEEK FOUR

Monday	Tuesday	Wednesday	Thursday	Friday	Saturday	Sunday
BREAKFAST	**BREAKFAST**	**BREAKFAST**	**BREAKFAST**	**BREAKFAST**	**BREAKFAST**	**BREAKFAST**
1 oz. Shredded Wheat 4 oz. nut milk or soy milk 4 oz. plant-based yogurt	1 oz. Shredded Wheat 4 oz. nut milk or soy milk 4 oz. plant-based yogurt	1 oz. Shredded Wheat 4 oz. nut milk or soy milk 4 oz. plant-based yogurt	1 oz. Shredded Wheat 4 oz. nut milk or soy milk 4 oz. plant-based yogurt	1 oz. Shredded Wheat 4 oz. nut milk or soy milk 4 oz. plant-based yogurt	1 oz. Shredded Wheat 4 oz. nut milk or soy milk 4 oz. plant-based yogurt	1 oz. Shredded Wheat 4 oz. nut milk or soy milk 4 oz. plant-based yogurt
6 oz. mixed berries	6 oz. mixed berries	6 oz. mixed berries	6 oz. mixed berries	6 oz. mixed berries	6 oz. mixed berries	6 oz. mixed berries
LUNCH	**LUNCH**	**LUNCH**	**LUNCH**	**LUNCH**	**LUNCH**	**LUNCH**
Pickled Beets and Cucumbers 6 oz. beans ½ oz. hazelnuts	Pickled Beets and Cucumbers 4 oz. hummus topped with ½ oz. hazelnuts	Pickled Beets and Cucumbers 4 oz. hummus topped with ½ oz. hazelnuts	Roasted Asparagus with Kumquats and Almonds 4 oz. hummus	Cold Stuffed Pepper	Cold Stuffed Pepper	Cold Stuffed Pepper
6 oz. melon	6 oz. melon	6 oz. melon		6 oz. raspberries	6 oz. raspberries	6 oz. raspberries
DINNER	**DINNER**	**DINNER**	**DINNER**	**DINNER**	**DINNER**	**DINNER**
8 oz. mixed green salad with 1 tbsp chili powder, 6 oz. pinto beans, 2 oz. avocado, and 2 tbsp. balsamic vinegar	8 oz. mixed green salad with 1 tbsp chili powder, 6 oz. pinto beans, 2 oz. avocado, and 2 tbsp. balsamic vinegar	Mexican Cauliflower Rice with 6 oz. black beans	Mexican Cauliflower Rice with 6 oz. black beans	Susan's Tasty Tofu Roasted Enchilada Vegetables	Moroccan Carrot Bowl	Moroccan Carrot Bowl
Basic Roasted Vegetables for All Seasons	Basic Roasted Vegetables for All Seasons	8 oz. roasted asparagus	8 oz. roasted asparagus	8 oz. salad topped with 2 oz. salsa	8 oz. roasted asparagus	8 oz. roasted asparagus

Whole-Food Plant-Based Weekly Meal Plan

AUTUMN
WEEK ONE

Monday	Tuesday	Wednesday	Thursday	Friday	Saturday	Sunday
BREAKFAST	**BREAKFAST**	**BREAKFAST**	**BREAKFAST**	**BREAKFAST**	**BREAKFAST**	**BREAKFAST**
1 oz. Ezekiel Cereal 4 oz. plant-based milk 1 oz. sunflower seeds 1 apple	1 oz. Ezekiel Cereal 4 oz. plant-based milk 1 oz. sunflower seeds 1 apple	1 oz. Ezekiel Cereal 4 oz. plant-based milk 1 oz. sunflower seeds 1 apple	1 oz. Ezekiel Cereal 4 oz. plant-based milk 1 oz. sunflower seeds 1 apple	1 oz. Ezekiel Cereal 4 oz. plant-based milk 1 oz. sunflower seeds 1 apple	1 oz. Ezekiel Cereal 4 oz. plant-based milk 1 oz. sunflower seeds 1 apple	1 oz. Ezekiel Cereal 4 oz. plant-based milk 1 oz. sunflower seeds 1 apple
LUNCH	**LUNCH**	**LUNCH**	**LUNCH**	**LUNCH**	**LUNCH**	**LUNCH**
6 oz. mixed green salad tossed with 1 tbsp chili powder 6 oz. beans 2 oz. avocado 2 oz. salsa 6 oz. berries	6 oz. mixed green salad tossed with 1 tbsp chili powder 6 oz. beans 2 oz. avocado 2 oz. salsa 6 oz. berries	6 oz. mixed green salad tossed with 1 tbsp chili powder 6 oz. beans 2 oz. avocado 2 oz. salsa 6 oz. berries	Fresh Corn and Black Bean Salad 1 banana	Fresh Corn and Black Bean Salad 1 banana	Fresh Corn and Black Bean Salad 1 banana	Pickled Beets and Cucumbers 6 oz. white beans 2 oz. avocado 6 oz. berries
DINNER	**DINNER**	**DINNER**	**DINNER**	**DINNER**	**DINNER**	**DINNER**
4 oz. vegan sausage 6 oz. salad	Mediterranean Chopped Salad	Mediterranean Chopped Salad	Mediterranean Chopped Salad	Chipotle Vegan Sausage and White Bean Stew ½ oz. nuts	Chipotle Vegan Sausage and White Bean Stew ½ oz. nuts	Chipotle Vegan Sausage and White Bean Stew ½ oz. nuts
8 oz. roasted Brussels sprouts	Pickled Beets	Pickled Beets	Pickled Beets	8 oz. roasted broccoli	8 oz. roasted broccoli	8 oz. roasted broccoli

AUTUMN
WEEK TWO

Monday	Tuesday	Wednesday	Thursday	Friday	Saturday	Sunday
BREAKFAST	**BREAKFAST**	**BREAKFAST**	**BREAKFAST**	**BREAKFAST**	**BREAKFAST**	**BREAKFAST**
6 oz. beans 4 oz. cooked oatmeal 1 apple	6 oz. beans 4 oz. cooked oatmeal 1 apple	6 oz. beans 4 oz. cooked oatmeal 1 apple	6 oz. beans 4 oz. cooked oatmeal 1 apple	6 oz. beans 4 oz. cooked oatmeal 1 apple	6 oz. beans 4 oz. cooked oatmeal 1 apple	6 oz. beans 4 oz. cooked oatmeal 1 apple
LUNCH	**LUNCH**	**LUNCH**	**LUNCH**	**LUNCH**	**LUNCH**	**LUNCH**
Steamed Kale and Lentil Bowl	Steamed Kale and Lentil Bowl	Steamed Kale and Lentil Bowl	Steamed Kale and Lentil Bowl	6 oz. cooked white beans 6 oz. salad Miso Tahini Dressing 1 apple	6 oz. cooked white beans 6 oz. salad Miso Tahini Dressing 1 apple	6 oz. cooked white beans 6 oz. salad Miso Tahini Dressing 1 apple
DINNER	**DINNER**	**DINNER**	**DINNER**	**DINNER**	**DINNER**	**DINNER**
African Bean Stew	African Bean Stew	Moroccan Carrot Bowl	Moroccan Carrot Bowl	Very Veggie Chili	Very Veggie Chili	Very Veggie Chili
		8 oz. Basic Roasted Vegetables for All Seasons	8 oz. Basic Roasted Vegetables for All Seasons			

Whole-Food Plant-Based Weekly Meal Plan

AUTUMN
WEEK THREE

Monday	Tuesday	Wednesday	Thursday	Friday	Saturday	Sunday
BREAKFAST	**BREAKFAST**	**BREAKFAST**	**BREAKFAST**	**BREAKFAST**	**BREAKFAST**	**BREAKFAST**
Beans, Sweet Potatoes, and Apples, Oh My!	Beans, Sweet Potatoes, and Apples, Oh My!	Beans, Sweet Potatoes, and Apples, Oh My!	Beans, Sweet Potatoes, and Apples, Oh My!	Beans, Sweet Potatoes, and Apples, Oh My!	Beans, Sweet Potatoes, and Apples, Oh My!	Beans, Sweet Potatoes, and Apples, Oh My!
LUNCH	**LUNCH**	**LUNCH**	**LUNCH**	**LUNCH**	**LUNCH**	**LUNCH**
Pickled Beets and Cucumbers 6 oz. white beans 2 oz. avocado 6 oz. berries	Fresh Corn and Black Bean Salad 1 banana	Fresh Corn and Black Bean Salad 1 banana	Fresh Corn and Black Bean Salad 1 banana	6 oz. mixed green salad tossed with 1 tbsp chili powder 6 oz. beans 2 oz. avocado, 2 oz. salsa 6 oz. berries	6 oz. mixed green salad tossed with 1 tbsp chili powder 6 oz. beans 2 oz. avocado, 2 oz. salsa 6 oz. berries	6 oz. mixed green salad tossed with 1 tbsp chili powder 6 oz. beans 2 oz. avocado, 2 oz. salsa 6 oz. berries
DINNER	**DINNER**	**DINNER**	**DINNER**	**DINNER**	**DINNER**	**DINNER**
Latin Stuffed Peppers	Latin Stuffed Peppers	Latin Stuffed Peppers	African Bean Stew	Chipotle Vegan Sausage and White Bean Stew ½ oz. nuts	Chipotle Vegan Sausage and White Bean Stew ½ oz. nuts	6 oz. cooked beans 6 oz. roasted butternut squash
				8 oz. roasted eggplant	8 oz. roasted eggplant	8 oz. salad Hummus Dressing

AUTUMN
WEEK FOUR

Monday	Tuesday	Wednesday	Thursday	Friday	Saturday	Sunday
BREAKFAST	**BREAKFAST**	**BREAKFAST**	**BREAKFAST**	**BREAKFAST**	**BREAKFAST**	**BREAKFAST**
4 oz. cooked oatmeal 6 oz. plant-based yogurt ½ oz. ground flax 6 oz. pomegranate	4 oz. cooked oatmeal 6 oz. plant-based yogurt ½ oz. ground flax 6 oz. pomegranate	4 oz. cooked oatmeal 6 oz. plant-based yogurt ½ oz. ground flax 6 oz. pomegranate	4 oz. cooked oatmeal 6 oz. plant-based yogurt ½ oz. ground flax 6 oz. pomegranate	4 oz. cooked oatmeal 6 oz. plant-based yogurt ½ oz. ground flax 6 oz. pomegranate	4 oz. cooked oatmeal 6 oz. plant-based yogurt ½ oz. ground flax 6 oz. pomegranate	4 oz. cooked oatmeal 6 oz. plant-based yogurt ½ oz. ground flax 6 oz. pomegranate
LUNCH	**LUNCH**	**LUNCH**	**LUNCH**	**LUNCH**	**LUNCH**	**LUNCH**
6 oz. cooked white beans 6 oz. salad Miso Tahini Dressing 1 apple	6 oz. cooked white beans 6 oz. salad Hummus Dressing 1 apple	6 oz. cooked white beans 6 oz. salad Hummus Dressing 1 apple	Texas Caviar 6 oz. berries	Texas Caviar 6 oz. berries	Texas Caviar 6 oz. berries	6 oz. black beans 6 oz. salad topped with 1 tbsp chili powder 2 tbsp salsa 2 oz. diced avocado 1 apple
DINNER	**DINNER**	**DINNER**	**DINNER**	**DINNER**	**DINNER**	**DINNER**
6 oz. roasted butternut squash 6 oz. cooked beans 2 oz. hummus	Moroccan Carrot Bowl	Moroccan Carrot Bowl	Chipotle Vegan Sausage and White Bean Stew ½ oz. nuts	Chipotle Vegan Sausage and White Bean Stew ½ oz. nuts	Latin Stuffed Peppers	Latin Stuffed Peppers
8 oz. salad	8 oz. roasted Brussels sprouts	8 oz. roasted Brussels sprouts	8 oz. roasted broccoli	8 oz. roasted broccoli		

MOLLY DOOGAN

STARTING DATE **July 25, 2017**

HEAVIEST WEIGHT **220 pounds**

STARTING WEIGHT **214 pounds**

GOAL WEIGHT ACHIEVED **September 7, 2018**

CURRENT WEIGHT **110 pounds**

HEIGHT **5'3"**

For 40 years the dysfunctional cycle of sugar/flour addiction and mastering restricting/bingeing kept my weight in a constant yo-yo. Initially it was a 5- to 10-pound flux, then 15 to 20 pounds, escalating until I bounced between 163 and 220-plus. Food became my nemesis—a mysterious code I was unable to crack—trying to figure out what, when, and how much to eat. I spent money, time, and endless energy on programs, therapists, nutritionists, alternative medicine, and even meditation looking for the answers. I tried everything short of surgery to right-size my body. With every effort and every miserable failure I was left feeling demoralized and sick—physically, mentally, emotionally, and spiritually.

Now, even though I eat similar meals day in/day out, I still write my daily food plan every evening. It brings me peace because I never know when a crazy day at work or active weekend is going to deplete my willpower, rendering me unable to make the best nutritional decisions. I learned to write a four- to five-day food plan outline, inventory my cupboards, and create a grocery shopping list (another novel idea!). Sundays I batch-cook roasted vegetables, grill proteins, and prepare chopped salad. This makes it super simple to pull together and pack or reheat a meal. When making plans to eat out, I research restaurants and menus in advance, determining my best choices and setting myself up for success.

These days my food is nutritious, delicious, and I thoroughly ENJOY eating. My family and friends think it is hilarious that I volunteered for the BLE cookbook team as my (prior) lack of culinary skills was well-known. Yes, now I'm happy and thin—I've released 110 pounds. However, for me, FREE—maintaining a quiet brain and peace with food—is the truly priceless surprise of the program. I'm so grateful I'm navigating the dance of maintenance with confidence and inspiring others to discover this amazing solution.

Brief Parting Words

*T*ruth be told, I never wanted to write a cookbook. In fact, a while back I put out a video blog explaining exactly why there would never be a Bright Line Eating cookbook—too much focus on the food, when this program isn't really about the food—it's about breaking free from food and finally *living life*. But the voices of people doing Bright Line Eating convinced me otherwise. It became clear that if I didn't put out a cookbook, some subset of people in our community would struggle with a too long on-ramp as they tried to sort out what to eat, or buy a fake BLE cookbook some charlatan is selling online (yes, they exist) and become entirely misled about how BLE works, or they'd simply give up and quit.

So I acquiesced and embarked on this epic project. A year or so later, much to my surprise, the experience of compiling this book has left me feeling really proud and excited. The thousands of BLE founders who first started doing this program, pulling themselves up by their bootstraps, really have stumbled on some helpful, unique, and simple ways to prepare Bright Line Eating meals, and now we can all benefit from their collective wisdom.

And so. Here you are, *you*, at the end of this not-so-typical cookbook, about to embark on the next phase of your BLE journey. The analogy that comes to mind is that you are leaving behind far too many years of being bound to earth in a body that weighs too much to move freely and instead you are now learning to fly a plane. Initially it will seem like a daunting task, but remember, thousands of other people were once exactly where you are now and they've mastered it. You will, too. First, with the help of all the information contained in this book, you'll get it off the runway. Then, over the next few months, as you attain automaticity and move food decisions out of the front of your brain, you'll get it up to cruising altitude. Once there, in a year or so, you will be able to relax in your newfound skill set, soaring along in a right-sized body.

But just as with flying a plane, that doesn't mean you'll get complacent or take your eyes off the control panel. You will always be flying this plane—reading the information coming in and making necessary adjustments. Here are some thoughts to keep you aloft.

CURIOSITY

I have mentioned a few times that I invite you to be a scientist when it comes to finding the right foods to include in your plan, and the foods you might need to let fall by the wayside. (Nut butters come to mind here.) But I have found over the years that the best way to handle being a Bright Lifer is to stay curious about all of it. No matter what is cropping up as life gets life-y, be curious. It's all helpful. If you find that suddenly old temptations are rearing their ugly heads, or cravings, or food thoughts, or even breaks in your Lines, simply get curious.

What is your control panel telling you? Do you need to resimplify your food? Do you need more support? Have you recently added a new element into the mix that is throwing you off? Has a bakery opened on your route to work? You may be walking by thinking, *Not My Food*, but those smells could be throwing your lizard brain into a frenzy. Maybe you need to change your route. Another example: Some parents can't have a pot of starch on the table for their kids at dinner. They need to have their spouse dish it up from the kitchen. If you are having trouble sticking to your plan, give yourself permission to get curious and change up whatever is in your environment that is throwing off your peace.

Or perhaps it's not about food at all. Are you sliding off track with your habits and your support? Do a spot-check: Are you writing down your food the night before? Using your Nightly Checklist Sheet? Reaching out to the community to help you stay on track? To keep your plane on course, keep reading the instrument panel and making adjustments. When those headwinds come, try not to think, *Darn!* Instead think, *Huh. Let's check that out.* And, if things feel really wonky, it might be time to take another look at your deepest BLE identity.

COMMITMENT

Doing this as a diet will only work for so long. Your deep commitment to be a person who doesn't eat addictively over anything needs to be nurtured and renewed all the time. It is your inner commitment that will carry you through all the turbulence—births, deaths, divorce, illness, work stress, moving. Consider a ritual or affirmation that reinforces that commitment. Mantras are so powerful. "Don't eat no matter what; no matter what, just don't eat." "That's not my food, that's poison to me." "Don't give up what you want most for what you think you want right now."

Also remember that a new identity takes time to form and solidify. Day by day *become* someone who does this. You will soar above the turbulence when you make the shift from "I do Bright Line Eating" to "I *am* a Bright Lifer."

I leave you with this thought: Embrace the paradox. If you surrender and follow the structure of the Bright Lines, you will find liberation on the other side. Commit to the work of getting yourself set up so that ultimately this feels like no work at all. Let go of what you thought food was to discover what food *can be*.

Lastly, we are a community here to help you. BLE is about so much more than the food. People "come for the vanity and stay for the sanity." It's an adventure of rediscovering the fullness of life, growing and stretching, and connecting with others in an ever more deep and satisfying way. It never ends. It never gets old. Find us online and make use of our wisdom. Lean on us. Let us cheer you on through this huge change.

And know that whatever doubts you are having right now, I know you can do this. You are no different from the thousands of people who have lost all their excess weight and kept it off. They mastered this new way of eating—and you can, too.

Welcome.

We are so glad you are here.

Endnotes

Introduction

1. A. Fildes, et al., "Probability of an Obese Person Attaining Normal Body Weight: Cohort Study Using Electronic Health Records," *American Journal of Public Health* 105, no. 9 (September 2015): E54–E59. doi: 10.2105/AJPH.2015.302773.

2. Centers for Disease Control and Prevention, National Center for Health Statistics, *Health, United States, 2017: With Special Feature on Mortality*, Table 53: "Selected health conditions and risk factors, by age: United States, selected years 1988–1994 through 2015–2016," https://www.cdc.gov/nchs/hus/contents2017.htm#Table_053.

3. A. C. Skinner, et al., "Prevalence of Obesity and Severe Obesity in U.S. Children, 1999–2016," *Pediatrics* 141, no. 3 (March 2018): e20173459. doi: 10.1542/peds.2017-3459.

4. Centers for Disease Control and Prevention, *National Diabetes Statistics Report*, 2017, https://www.cdc.gov/diabetes/data/statistics/statistics-report.html.

5. F. A. Fakorede, M.D., "Increasing Awareness This National Diabetes Month Can Save Limbs and Lives," *AJMC* Managed Markets Network, published November 29, 2018, https://www.ajmc.com/contributor/foluso-fakorede/2018/11/increasing-awareness-this-national-diabetes-month-can-save-limbs-and-lives.

6. M. Heron, "Deaths: Leading causes for 2016," *National Vital Statistics Reports* 67, no 6. (July 26, 2018), https://www.cdc.gov/nchs/data/nvsr/nvsr67/nvsr67_06.pdf.

Chapter 1

1. K. D. Vohs, et al., "Making Choices Impairs Subsequent Self-Control: A Limited Resource Account of Decision Making, Self-Regulation, and Active Initiative," *Journal of Personality and Social Psychology* 94, no. 5 (May 2008): 883–898. doi: 10.1037/0022-3514.94.5.883.

2. M. T. Gailliot, et al., "Self-Control Relies on Glucose as a Limited Energy source: Willpower Is More Than a Metaphor" *Journal of Personality and Social Psychology* 92, no. 2 (February 2007): 325–336. doi: 10.1037/0022-3514.92.2.325.

3. A. M. Ingalls, et al., "Obese, a New Mutation in the House Mouse," *Obesity Research* 4, no. 1 (January 1996): 101. doi: 10.1002/j.1550-8528.1996.tb00519.x.

4. Y. Zhang, et al., "Positional Cloning of the Mouse Obese Gene and Its Human Homolog," *Nature* 372, no. 6505 (December 1994): 425–432. doi: 10.1038/372425a0.

5. R. H. Lustig, et al., "Obesity, Leptin Resistance, and the Effects of Insulin Reduction," *International Journal of Obesity* 28, no. 10 (October 2004): 1344–1348. doi: 10.1038/sj.ijo.0802753.

6. O. Pinhas-Hamiel, et al., "Lipid and Insulin Levels in Obese Children: Changes with Age and Puberty," *Obesity* 15, no. 11 (2007): 2825–2831. doi: 10.1038/oby.2007.335.

7. J. M. Hanna and C. A. Hornick, "Use of Coca Leaf in Southern Peru: adaptation or Addiction," *Bulletin on Narcotics* 29, no. 1 (January–March 1977): 63–74, https://www.ncbi.nlm.nih.gov/pubmed/585582.

8. K. Verebey and M. S. Gold, "From Coca Leaves to Crack: The Effects of Dose and Routes of Administration in Abuse Liability," *Psychiatric Annals* 18, no. 9 (September 1988): 513–520. doi: 10.3928/0048-5713-19880901-06.

9. R. Lustig, *The Skinny on Obesity* (ep. 4): "Sugar—A Sweet Addiction," (May 8, 2012), retrieved from http://www.uctv.tv/shows/The-Skinny-on-Obesity-Ep-4-Sugar-A-Sweet-Addiction-23717.

10. J. E. Stewart, et al., "Oral Sensitivity to Fatty Acids, Food Consumption and BMI in Human Subjects," *British Journal of Nutrition* 104, no. 1 (July 2010): 145–152. doi: 10.1017/S0007114510000267.

11. E. Stice, et al., "Reward from Food Intake and Anticipated Food Intake to Obesity: A Functional Magnetic Resonance Imaging Study," *Journal of Abnormal Psychology* 117, no. 4 (November 2008): 924–935. doi: 10.1037/a0013600.

12. B. Wansink and J. Sobal, "Mindless Eating: The 200 Daily Food Decisions We Overlook," *Environment and Behavior* 39, no. 1 (January 1, 2007): 106–123. doi: 10.1177/0013916506295573.

13. Q. P. Wang, et al., "Sucralose Promotes Food Intake through NPY and a Neuronal Fasting Response," *Cell Metabolism* 24, no. 1 (July 12, 2016): 75–90. doi: 10.1016/j.cmet.2016.06.010.

14. Q. P. Wang, et al., "Non-nutritive Sweeteners Possess a Bacteriostatic Effect and Alter Gut Microbiota in Mice," *PLoS One* 13, no. 7 (July 5, 2018): e0199080. doi: 10.1371/journal.pone.0199080.

15. K. S. Juntunen, et al., "Postprandial Glucose, Insulin, and Incretin Responses to Grain Products in Healthy Subjects," *American Journal of Clinical Nutrition* 75, no. 2 (February 2002): 254–62. doi: 10.1093/ajcn/75.2.254.

16. E. M. Schulte, et al., "Which Foods May Be Addictive? The Roles of Processing, Fat Content, and Glycemic Load," *PLoS One* 10, no. 2 (February 18, 2015): e0117959. doi: 10.1371/journal.pone.0117959.

17. P. Lally, et al., "How Are Habits Formed: Modelling Habit Formation in the Real World," *European Journal of Social Psychology* 40, no. 6 (October 2010): 998–1009. doi: 10.1002/ejsp.674.

Chapter 2

1. A. Greene, "7 Things You Didn't Know About Your Taste Buds," *Woman's Day* (July 18, 2011), http://www.womansday.com/health-fitness/wellness/a5789/7-things-you-didnt-know-about-your-taste-buds-119709/.

2. M. K. Badman and J. S. Flier, "The Gut and Energy Balance: Visceral Allies in the Obesity Wars," *Science* 307, no. 5717 (March 25, 2005): 1909–1914. doi: 10.1126/science.1109951.

3. G. Blackburn, "Effect of Degree of Weight Loss on Health Benefits," *Obesity Research* 3, no. 211S-216S (September 3, 1995). doi: 10.1002/j.1550-8528.1995.tb00466.x.

4. R. Voelker, "Partially Hydrogenated Oils Are Out," *JAMA* 314, no. 5 (August 4, 2015): 443. doi: 10.1001/jama.2015.8387.

5. R. M. Reynolds, et al., "Disorders of Sodium Balance," *BMJ: British Medical Journal* 332, no. 7543 (March 23, 2006): 702–705. doi: 10.1136/bmj.332.7543.702.

6. B. R. Schienker, et al., "The Impact of Self-Presentations on Self-Appraisals and Behavior: The Power of Public Commitment," *Personality and Social Psychology Bulletin* 20, no. 1 (February 1, 1994): 20–33. doi: 10.1177/0146167294201002.

7. P. U. Nyer and S. Dellande, "Public Commitment as a Motivator for Weight Loss," *Psychology and Marketing* 27, no. 1 (January 2010): 1–12. doi: 10.1002/mar.20316.

8. C. P. Herman and D. Mack, "Restrained and Unrestrained Eating," *Journal of Personality* 43, no. 4 (1975): 647–660. doi: 10.1111/j.1467-6494.1975.tb00727.x.

Chapter 3

1. S. J. Guyenet, Ph.D., *The Hungry Brain: Outsmarting the Instincts That Make Us Overeat* (New York City: Flatiron Books, 2017).

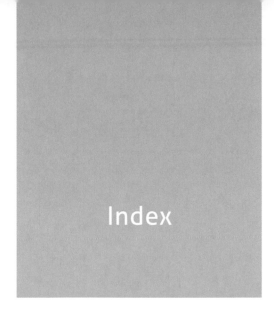

Index

NOTE:

Page references in italics refer to photos.

Sauces, and Salsas; Food plan ("plan"); Omnivore's weekly meal plan; Perfect Plates; Tips, tricks, and techniques; Warm Bowls (Dinner Domain); Whole-food plant-based weekly meal plan

Adiposity Set Point and, 60–61

automaticity for, 15–17

"before" pictures, 43

BLE Boot Camps, xii–xiii, 17–19, 63

Brain's role and, 4, 7–11

Bright Lifers, overview, xiii

Bright Lines, adhering to, 36

Bright Lines, defined, 12–15

commitment to, 324

curiosity and experimenting for, 323

eliminating sugar and flour with, 11–14

Food Freedom Quiz, xi–xii

Four S's of, 48–50

as identity, 51

insatiable hunger and, 5

inspiration for, 321–322

invitation to, 19

leptin and, 6

as no-exercise plan, 17–19

overpowering cravings with, 6–7

overview, ix–xix

reducing stress for, 17

simple food for, 61–65

solving a "food problem" vs., 59–60

support community for, 46–47

surrendering to, 65

Susceptibility Scale, xii, 13

willpower and, 3–5, 15–17

Broccoli
Broccoli Slaw and Roasted Corn Salad, 180, 181

"Cream" of Broccoli Soup, 216, 217

storing, 113

Brussels sprouts, storing, 113

"Bunny slippers," for stress reduction, 17

C

Cabbage Stir-Fry, Hamburger and, 206, 207

Caffeine, 40–41

Caprese Salad, 167

Carol, Julia, 109, 111, 254, 261, 265, 272

Carrots
Moroccan Carrot Bowl, 192, 193

storing, 112

Cauliflower
Cauliflower Fried Rice, 200, 201

Mexican Cauliflower Rice, 132, 133

storing, 113

Celery, storing, 112

Cellular healing (autophagy), 15

Cereal. See also Grains
about, 27

Cottage Cheese, Cereal, and Berries, 78, 79

Champion, Kimberly, 259, 269

Charred Green Beans, 119

Checklist, for next day (Nightly Checklist), 45, 50

Cheeses
Caprese Salad, 167

Cheese and Rice Omelet, 90, 91

Cottage Cheese, Cereal, and Berries, 78, 79

Eggplant Parmesan, 160, 161

Herbed Blueberries with Goat Cheese, 153

Nondairy Parmesan Cheese, 230

plant-based, 30

Ricotta Oats in a Jar, 88, 89

Chia Pudding, 84, 85

Chicken
Chicken and Apple Slaw, 190, 191

Chicken and Vegetable Soup, 222, 223

Acknowledgments

*I*t is almost absurd that my name is on the cover when this has been such a labor of love for the Bright Lifers community, whose contribution of recipes, tips, tricks, techniques, life stories, and honest and vulnerable advice has made this book what it is.

I must start by thanking our contributors, Betsy Meynardie, Cindy Rinaman Marsch, Denise Fitzsimmons, Dina Grossman, Jennifer Doonan, Karen Griffin, Linda Schmitz, Lisa Parrott, Louanne LaRoche, Masha Vujanovic, Laurie Avenell Olson, Irina Lee, Molly Doogan, Jana Allen, Nathan M. Denkin, Dee Holland-Vogt, Lisa Houser, Samantha Hughes, Anita Wicks Luther, Shanda McGrew, Sonja Schneider, Cindy Smith, Mary Reisz, Charlotte Coit, Susan Cook, Amanda Michelle Albright, Beth Syverson, Erin Wallace, Marian Walters, Debby Edwards, Evelyn Zoecklein, Julie Boyd Smith, Josie Colicchia, Shobha Tallapaka, Maria Ines Segret, Sharon Mack, Nikki Van-DenHeuvel, Valerie Proctor-Conner, Louise Giffels, Evelyn Ziegler, Heidi Stallman, Julia Carol, Ellen Eichen Weinman, Cathy Johnson, Terry Mandel, LeeAnn Thompson, Sue Gaulke, Ronald Mackenberg, Natalie Quinn, Ruth G. Poley, Lisa Erickson,

Ruth Martin, Amy Lampert, Kathy Lafontaine Hashley, Leslee Feiwus, Elaine Taylor, Lynda Dahl, Lillian Smith, Beth Kerrick, Kathy Hettinger, C.J. Hast, Lisa Branic, Kathryn Doran, Susan Gilbert Zencka, Julia Harold, Katie Mae, Vicki Weik, Teri Meggers, Mary Mazzone, Lynn Powers, Nancy Wolf, Gaye Welton, Sondra McNair, Michele Mariscal, Kimberly Champion, Lisa Rowe, Kallie Kendle, Chris Southwick, Amelia Jordan, Maitreyi Margie Wilsman, Kent Rappleye, Jodi Maile, Jodie McDowell, Michelle Pecharich, Ellen Moyer, Mary Judkins, and Peggy Mowry.

Also, big thanks to the over 400 Bright Lifers who participated in the Facebook cookbook volunteer group and the over 200 Bright Lifers who participated in the Facebook recipe testing group.

Bright Light Eating team members jumped in at so many points and provided heroic assistance to get this book completed. My enormous gratitude to Gina Blancato, Nadia Briones, JoAnn Campbell-Rice, Lynn Coulston, Christine Davis, Angela Denby, Julia Harold, Laura Hudson, Samantha Hughes, Sonja Johansen, Marianne Marsh, Jenn Moon, Linden Morris Delrio, Crystal Ruzicka, Angela Simpson, Erica Stuart, and Sanz Su'a.

For your tireless proofreading acumen, thank you Sharon Cheek, Eileen Lass of The Lass Word Proofreading and Editing, and Jackie Montarra.

Nathan M. Denkin, Ph.D., deserves special recognition for his ever-appreciated work chasing down references and citations and assisting with our calculations.

Two books in and many more to come, I must thank my exceptional publishing dream team. I love working with you.

My agent extraordinaire, Lucinda Blumenfeld, for her tireless advocacy.

Ashley Bernardi, our PR guru, who makes spreading the word and helping more people so much fun.

Sally Mason-Swaab, Patty Gift, Reid Tracy, and the entire team at Hay House, who have given Bright Line eating such a wonderful home; you are truly a publishing company unlike any other.

And finally, of course, Nicola Kraus and Julia Carol. You know this book is yours. Thank you so much for your tireless work from beginning to end bringing this project to life. My gratitude and appreciation are boundless.

About the Author

Susan Peirce Thompson, Ph.D., is an Adjunct Associate Professor of Brain and Cognitive Sciences at the University of Rochester, an expert in the psychology of eating, and the *New York Times* best-selling author of *Bright Line Eating: The Science of Living Happy, Thin, and Free*. She is President of the Institute for Sustainable Weight Loss and the founder and CEO of Bright Line Eating Solutions, a company dedicated to helping people achieve long-term, sustainable weight loss.

Website:
BrightLineEating.com

HAY HOUSE TITLES
of Related Interest

YOU CAN HEAL YOUR LIFE, *the movie,*
starring Louise Hay & Friends

(available as a 1-DVD program, an expanded 2-DVD set, and an online streaming video)

Learn more at www.hayhouse.com/louise-movie

THE SHIFT, *the movie,*
starring Dr. Wayne W. Dyer

(available as a 1-DVD program, an expanded 2-DVD set, and an online streaming video)

Learn more at www.hayhouse.com/the-shift-movie

All of the above are available at your local bookstore,
or may be ordered by contacting Hay House (see next page).

We hope you enjoyed this Hay House book. If you'd like to receive our online catalog featuring additional information on Hay House books and products, or if you'd like to find out more about the Hay Foundation, please contact:

Hay House, Inc., P.O. Box 5100, Carlsbad, CA 92018-5100
(760) 431-7695 or (800) 654-5126
(760) 431-6948 (fax) or (800) 650-5115 (fax)
www.hayhouse.com® • www.hayfoundation.org

• • •

Published in Australia by:
Hay House Australia Pty. Ltd.,
18/36 Ralph St., Alexandria NSW 2015
Phone: 612-9669-4299 • *Fax:* 612-9669-4144 • www.hayhouse.com.au

Published in the United Kingdom by:
Hay House UK, Ltd.,
The Sixth Floor, Watson House, 54 Baker Street, London W1U 7BU
Phone: +44 (0)20 3927 7290 • *Fax:* +44 (0)20 3927 7291 • www.hayhouse.co.uk

Published in India by:
Hay House Publishers India,
Muskaan Complex, Plot No. 3, B-2, Vasant Kunj, New Delhi 110 070
Phone: 91-11-4176-1620 • *Fax:* 91-11-4176-1630 • www.hayhouse.co.in

• • •

Access New Knowledge.

Anytime. Anywhere.

Learn and evolve at your own pace
with the world's leading experts.

www.hayhouseU.com

Free e-newsletters
from Hay House, the Ultimate
Resource for Inspiration

Be the first to know about Hay House's free downloads, special offers, giveaways, contests, and more!

 Get exclusive excerpts from our latest releases and videos from *Hay House Present Moments*.

 Our *Digital Products Newsletter* is the perfect way to stay up-to-date on our latest discounted eBooks, featured mobile apps, and Live Online and On Demand events.

 Learn with real benefits! *HayHouseU.com* is your source for the most innovative online courses from the world's leading personal growth experts. Be the first to know about new online courses and to receive exclusive discounts.

 Enjoy uplifting personal stories, how-to articles, and healing advice, along with videos and empowering quotes, within *Heal Your Life*.

Sign Up Now!

Get inspired, educate yourself, get a complimentary gift, and share the wisdom!

Visit www.hayhouse.com/newsletters to sign up today!

 HAY HOUSE

 HAYHOUSE RADIO *radio for your soul®*

 HAYHOUSE online learning

Tune In to
Hay House Radio—
Radio for Your Soul

HAY HOUSE RADIO offers inspirational and personalized advice from our best-selling authors, including Anthony William, Dr. Christiane Northrup, Doreen Virtue, James Van Praagh, and many more!

Enjoy **FREE** access to life-changing audio 24/7 on HayHouseRadio.com, and with the Hay House Radio mobile app.

Listen anytime to the Hay House Radio archives of over 13,000 episodes (and more added daily!) with a Hay House Radio All Access Pass.

Learn more at www.HayHouseRadio.com